AVIA
——— in ———
DONCASTER
1909-1992

Geoffrey Oakes

Geoffrey Oakes

First Published 1995

Printed by Askew Design & Print
Heavens Walk, Ten Pound Walk, Doncaster

IBSN 0 9524838 0 7

Published by G. H. Oakes
42 Cranwell Road, Cantley, Doncaster DN4 6EP
Telephone: 01302 538524

AVIATION

in

DONCASTER

1909-1992

Doncaster has been famous in the twentieth century for two major industries, railways and coal. There should have been a third, aviation.

In 1909, with the active and financial support of the town fathers, Doncaster held the UK's first-ever air display and for the next 83 years, to a greater or lesser degree, the town has played a part in the country's aviation history.

During the first world war, Doncaster had a Royal Flying Corps (RFC) station. In the second, there were airfields at Finningley, Lindholme, Bircotes (just north of Bawtry) and Doncaster; Bawtry Hall was the headquarters of 1 Group Bomber Command; and a factory at Doncaster Airport built and repaired aircraft.

After the war, Doncaster County Borough Council granted the Freedom of the Town to 616 (South Yorkshire) Squadron RAAF (Royal Auxiliary Air Force). After the amalgamation of local Councils in 1974, this 'Freedom' was not continued (how can you <u>un</u>freedom an RAF squadron?). However, to even things up, the Freedom was granted to RAF Finningley.

By 1994, all RAF establishments in Doncaster had closed, except for Finningley, for many years home to Europe's largest air display - and even Finningley was under sentence of death. The aerodrome that had served the RFC in the first world war was covered with housing, the Armthorpe airfield had returned to farming, and Doncaster Airport had become the home of the Dome and other leisure activities, not to mention a super store.

Nowhere now is there any mention of Doncaster's aviation past. Many people who work or live on the various sites are unaware of it. I hope this book will come as an interesting surprise.

CHAPTER 1

1909-1934

A dream as old as man was fulfilled at 10.35 am on December 17, 1903 when Orville Wright made the world's first controlled, powered flight. Wright's machine, called 'The Flyer', took off from a 40 foot long wooden rail laid out on level ground at Kill Devil Hill, Kitty Hawk, North Carolina and flew for 120 feet. The flight lasted 12 seconds. Other flights followed on the same day, with his brother Wilbur flying for 59 seconds and covering 852 feet.

The first powered flight in Europe took place nearly three years later on September 13, 1906 from a field near Paris - although the pilot was a Brazilian, Alberto Santos-Dumont. He flew for 20 feet at a height of two feet. A month later he flew further and higher, 197 feet at a height of ten feet, to win a prize of 3,000 French francs presented by Ernest Archdeacon, a wealthy Irish lawyer who had become President of the Aero-Club de France.

The first (partly) British flight was made by Henri (sometimes Henry) Farman, a naturalised Frenchman, the son of the Paris correspondent of the London Standard. After no fewer than 255 attempts, he eventually flew for a distance of 262 feet from a field at Issy-les-Moulineaux on September 30, 1907. On October 26, 1907, he flew for 2,530 feet. The first passenger flight in Europe was made, again in Paris, on March 28th, 1908 when Leon Delagrange carried Henry Farman in his biplane, 'Voison'.

The first sustained flight in Britain was by an American, Samuel F. Cody - no relation to William F. (Buffalo Bill) Cody. On October 16th, 1908 at Farnborough, Hampshire, he flew for 1391 feet at a height of up to 30 feet before crashing. In February 1909 the first aerodrome ever to be built in Britain was opened - at Leysdown on the Isle of Sheppey.

The world's first aviation meeting was held in France at Rheims on August 22, 1909 - with over 200,000 French francs as prizes. Among the 500,000 spectators were the wife of the former US President Teddy Roosevelt, the future British prime minister David Lloyd George and the press tycoon Lord Northcliffe, publisher of the

Barry Thompson

7

Times and Daily Mail (though three years earlier, the Times Engineering Editor had written that 'Aviation is dangerous and doomed to failure!').

Meanwhile, arrangements were going ahead for the first ever air show in this country. It was to be held on the sands at Blackpool with the backing of the National Aero Club. Unfortunately, for them, they had competition - Doncaster. Some British and French enthusiasts, led by Monsieur Lambert, a millionaire from Spa in Belgium, had set up a syndicate to stage a British aviation meeting similar to the Rheims event. Several sites were considered. One of them was Doncaster and the syndicate combined business with pleasure by attending the 1909 St. Leger meeting.

Barry Thompson

Some of the aviators who took part in the 1909 Aviation Meeting   RAFM

They were impressed with the potential of Doncaster. They saw the 'straight' on the racecourse, a mile and a half long, and a grass-covered common surrounded by miles of flat open country. They also noted that the stands and enclosures could accommodate several hundred thousand spectators.

Doncaster was clearly the best choice. The syndicate approached the Corporation and were granted permission to use the racecourse. The

Corporation went even further and guaranteed £5,000 towards expenses.

The National Aero Club, a self-appointed body incidentally, was understandably piqued and pronounced a ban on the Doncaster meeting, threatening that any one who took part in the display

Cups awarded in competitions during the 1909 Aviation Meeting at Doncaster

RAFM

would be barred from other official displays. However, many of the

Delagrange in his Bleriot at the 1909 Air Display at Doncaster. Fellow air pioneer Le Blon looking on

W. Mills

foremost aviators of the time, including Cody, Delagrange, Farman, Sommer and Le Blon, declared that they would defy the ban. And they did.

The show opened at the racecourse on Friday, October 15, three days before the National Aero Club's proposed meeting at Blackpool. It lasted until October 23.

Edward Mines in his own aeroplane on the racecourse at the 1909 Aviation Meeting at Doncaster. Note the elaborate braking system.

Bruce/Leslie

9

An early twin engined aircraft built by M. Chauviere on the racecourse at the 1909 Aviation meeting at Doncaster. It is not known whether it ever flew.   Bruce/Leslie

The first day was washed out - persistent heavy rain left parts of the course water-logged and unusable. The rest of the meeting was highly successful. To keep the spectators informed, each of the main pilots was given a different flag. When a pilot was about to fly, his flag was displayed on a central pole. Flags with different designs showed the type of flight he hoped to make and the official programme explained what these designs meant.

Regrettably, the programme was printed in London, not locally, and one of the programme's sponsors exhorted people to buy a particular sort of dog food - some things have not changed.

Leon Delagrange in a Bleriot flying past grandstand during the 1909 Aviation Meeting at Doncaster   M. J. Cuttriss

The pilots taking part were paid for bringing their aircraft - Cody, for instance, got £2,000, a fabulous sum in those days. In addition there were cash prizes, and the trophies donated by the Doncaster Corporation (they presented the Doncaster Cup), local tradespeople, the Great Northern Railway and Doncaster's MP, Mr. C.N. Nicholson.

There was also the prize offered by the Daily Mail to the first British pilot in a British aeroplane who completed a circular mile flight. Cody was so keen to win it that he signed British naturalisation papers in front of the crowd, with the band playing both the Star Spangled Banner and the National Anthem. Unfortunately, he crashed his British Army Aeroplane No.1 whilst taxiing. In fact most of the aircraft taking part were damaged at one time or another. Le Blon and Captain Lovelace both crashed their

Harold Blackburn taking off from Green House Field, now the site of the Royal Infirmary, on Saturday 20th September 1913 with a fare paying passenger.

Bruce/Leslie

Bleriots near the crowds - Le Blon's machine was blown by a sudden gust of wind towards the shilling (5p) enclosure. Repairs were carried out in specially erected sheds built on the course alongside Bawtry Road, near the starting gate for the St. Leger.

But there were many triumphs. Delagrange set a new world speed record of 49.9 miles an hour and Sommer made a flight of 29 miles helping him to win the Doncaster Cup with a total flying distance of 136 miles 280 yards. He also won the Whitworth Cup for the greatest distance flown in one day, 38 miles.

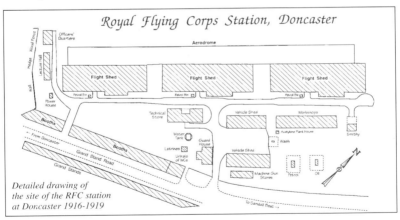

Detailed drawing of the site of the RFC station at Doncaster 1916-1919

The event was astonishingly popular with the people of Doncaster. They hung flags everywhere, and vast crowds turned up at the racecourse to watch, although in total only 80,000 actually paid. Some estimates put the <u>daily</u> attendance at over 100,000 - it was very easy to see events from outside the racecourse!

Special trains brought crowds from all over the country and from other parts of Europe. The Great Northern Railway cashed in on the bonanza

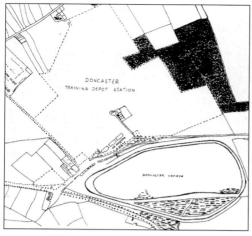

Area plan of RFC station at Doncaster 1916-1919 showing the extent of flying area from Town Moor Avenue almost to Thorne Road and covering a large part of the Intake estate.

(literally) by opening an exchange bureau for foreign currency at Doncaster Station. Trade in the town flourished, and all hotels were strained to meet the demand. The Danum Hotel, where the pilots stayed, engaged a staff of multi-lingual waiters. Even though the show lost money, the people of Doncaster were not worried. They had been privileged to enjoy a wonderful and historic week and the town had become famous throughout Europe.

It is sad to relate that within four years, aviation was to be the death of two of the pilots who performed at Doncaster. Delagrange was killed near Bordeaux in January 1910 and Cody crashed at Farnborough in August 1913 in the land version of a large sea plane that he hoped to develop into an aircraft to fly the Atlantic.

In 1910 another, grander, display was held at Doncaster, with aircraft flying over the town and circling the Parish Church. But it did not have the same impact as the previous year's event nor did it attract anything like the same number of spectators. Had Doncaster people become blasé about flying already?

Not really. In 1913 Harold Blackburn, son of a Carcroft school master, flew into Green House Field, now the site of the Doncaster Royal Infirmary, and gave pleasure flights - three guineas for a three-minute flight, five guineas for five minutes. The passenger had to

BE 2c fighter and trainer one of the types based at RFC Station Doncaster 1916-1919. It was an aircraft of this type that shot down a Zeppelin L-34 on 27/28 November 1916. The aircraft was based at Seaton Carew and flown by Lt. Pyott.

B. Robertson

SE5A fighter one of the types based at   B. Robertson
RFC Station Doncaster 1916-1919

indemnify the owner and pilot against any injury to himself during the flight. One of the passengers was W.E. Clark the founder of a Doncaster motor company of the same name. A later Managing Director of the company was Ralph Edwards whose father A.O. Edwards owned an aircraft called 'Grosvenor House', a De Havilland Comet. In 1934 the Comet, one of three taking part, won the 11,333 mile race from England to Australia, taking two days, 22 hours and 54 minutes. The race was held to mark the centenary of the state of Victoria.

Doncaster's place on the aviation map was confirmed during the first world war when, in 1916, a permanent aerodrome was opened by the Government for the Royal Flying Corps (RFC). It was sited to the north of the racecourse on the opposite side of what is now Leger Way and included what is now Intake. Three large Belfast hangars were built, each 200 ft by 64ft and similar in design to the hangars at Hendon, the home today of the Royal Air Force Museum.

Doncaster, like most RFC stations in this country, was intended for flying training only. Even when war had been declared, the thought that enemy aircraft would cross the seas with evil intent was never entertained. In fact it was not until the third year of war that German aircraft - Gothas - attempted to bomb England, and then only in the south. However, everyone had forgotten about Zeppelins.

The station came under the command of 6th Brigade, North East Area, 24 Group, 46th Wing for Home Defence and 16 Group, 8th Wing for training. The original plans had Doncaster as little more than a 'factory' for turning out squadrons for the mincing machine of the Western Front. The first units to come to Doncaster for training arrived on January 1, 1916. They were 15 RAS (Reserve Aeroplane Squadron) and 15 RS (Reserve Squadron). They had a mixed bag of aircraft - H. Farmans, Avro 504s and BE2cs.

In the previous year, 1915, the calm of the country had been

Avro 504 K fighter and trainer one of the types based   B. Robertson
at RFC Doncaster 1916-1919 and the only aircraft that
saw service in both world wars.

disturbed by the appearance of Zeppelins operating mainly from bases in Belgium and north west Germany. The War Office then directed that front-line fighters were to be based at Doncaster.

A small fighter detachment had been based for a few months in 1915 on the racecourse but had left before the RFC station opened. To meet the new threat, a detachment from 41 Squadron equipped with BE2cs was posted to Doncaster. When they left for their home base at Beverley, they were replaced by a detachment of 33 Squadron from Bramham Moor who stayed for a few months.

On the night of April 3/4, 1916, two Zeppelins set out to bomb London but were blown north and crossed the Yorkshire coast. Captain A. A. B. Thomson of 15 RAS took off at 23.00 hours from Doncaster in a BE2c to intercept them, but he failed to see the enemy and he himself crashed at Tealby near Market Rasen at 01.45 hours. Again on the night of May 2/3, there was a large-scale raid when more than a dozen Zeppelins crossed the coast. One of the Home Defence BE2cs was sent up from Doncaster to meet them, but though it flew for over an hour and a half, it failed to intercept.

These raids caused wide-spread fear and alarm and it was not until November 1916 that the northern squadrons had any success - when Lt. Pyott, operating out of Seaton Carew on Teesside and flying a BE2c, shot down Zeppelin L-34 near West Hartlepool.

Many Yorkshire towns and cities were on the receiving end of Zeppelin

BE2c of 15 RS after crashing   B. Robertson *Another view of the BE2c*   B. Robertson
into racecourse grandstand late 1916.   *which crashed into the Ladies Stand*
The passage way was later covered in and used   *at the racecourse late 1916.*
as a champagne and oyster bar.

raids. Leeds, Sheffield and Bradford were all attacked, although towns on the east coast suffered the most.

Meanwhile Doncaster continued its task of setting up and training new squadrons. 46 Reserve Squadron was formed on October 23, 1916 and it moved to Bramham Moor in December. It was followed by 80 Training Squadron, formed on January 1, 1917 as a Canadian unit. It

Sopwith Cuckoo built by Blackburn. This is the 5th production model based at Torpedo School at East Fortune. It is shown releasing its torpedo in the Firth of Forth 1919. Bruce/Leslie

moved to Camp Bordon, Canada after two months. Another Canadian unit, 90 Training Squadron, was formed in March and moved to Beverley in April. Between the two Canadian units, 82 Squadron was formed and was operating in France by the end of 1917. The two original squadrons were posted to Spittlegate near Grantham in September, 1917 and were replaced by 4 Reserve Squadron which stayed until July, 1918 when it was disbanded. The station then became the home of 41 and 49 Training Squadrons with 24 SE5As and 24 Avro 504s. These squadrons were amalgamated into 47 Training Depot and were the airfield's last occupants before it was closed in 1919.

Flying in those days was a dangerous business. On one terrible occasion, an Avro 504 crashed and caught fire without the pilot being able to escape and with bystanders utterly unable to help. Within minutes, another Avro 504 crashed on the road between the airfield and the racecourse. These were just two of the many accidents. Some of the dead aircrew are buried in the cemetery at Hyde Park.

There are few contemporary accounts of life at the RFC Station but a Lt. W.M. Fry has written about his stay at Doncaster in 1916 before the station was completed.

He arrived at the end of May after six weeks of elementary training with others of his course for advanced flying training to No. 15 RS which was commanded by Capt. J.E.A. Baldwin of the 8th Hussars later Air Marshal. The sergeants mess and other offices were in the racecourse buildings and the officers mess in what is now the Grand St. Leger Hotel. The hotel, then just a large house had been used, in peace time, by Lord Lonsdale for Leger week. The aircraft were Avros, Armstrong Whitworths and a few Be2c's. A number of the instructors were highly decorated officers on rest from France. The advanced training started on Avros followed by going solo on Armstrong Whitworths. Much of the training consisted of cross country flying together with ground lectures. The students could by and large choose where they wanted to fly but the exercise had to include at least 2 landings at other aerodromes. Their course had to be approved by their flight commander and the aircraft signed as fit for the flight. One of the most popular trips was to the old racecourse at Scarborough calling in at York, Catterick or Bramham Moor on the way back. The airfield at Scarborough was a mile or so from the town and run by the navy who provided transport, which always seemed to be Rolls-Royces. In Scarborough they had lunch in a hotel. They had little faith in their compasses and usually navigated by following the railway lines, most of them in the area led to Doncaster. When Lt. Fry made his first landing on the Knavesmire at York he had been told that it was a large flat area with plenty of room though no one had told him about the railings which he saw too late and he hit them. No one seemed to mind, just his flight commander telling him to be more careful next time. The people of Doncaster came in large numbers to watch the flying, though the pilots thought what they really wanted to see were crashes.

Some weekends, when there were more spectators, to fulfil their expectations the airmen took up a life sized dummy and threw it out and the ambulance men rushed out with a stretcher to collect the body. Flying pay was 8 shillings a day, and a second lieutenant earned just under 10 shillings a day, a very handsome wage for the time though the life span of a pilot at the front in France was only a matter of a few weeks. When the trainee had accumulated a specified number of hours and had reached the required standard he was awarded his wing's. There was no formal wing's parade, just the commanding officer announcing in the mess that certain pilots had passed and that was it. The next morning the newly qualified pilots appeared in the mess with their new wings and then off for a few days leave before leaving for France.

After only three years' active service, the apparently permanent airfield at Doncaster was closed. It was symptomatic of the feeling throughout the country ... the war's over, let's get on with living. The last thing the Government wanted to do was to spend money on the armed forces. All the services suffered and the RFC, now the Royal Air Force, was reduced from nearly 200 front line squadrons at the end of the war to one, plus a few others for training, all within the space of seven months.

But Doncaster had another aviation string to its bow - aircraft manufacture. The aircraft industry was in its infancy. There were few specialist companies, but the demand was huge and any firm that might be suitable was brought into aircraft production. One of these companies was Peglers of Doncaster who were skilled in the use of brass but had no experience in the manufacture of aircraft. They were awarded a contract to make 50 Sopwith Cuckoo torpedo carriers and production started in the latter part of the war. However, because of the firm's inexperience in airframe manufacture and also because of changes in design, the contract was reduced to 20 aircraft and the balance was taken over by Blackburn

Aircraft of Brough, Hull. Only one aircraft was actually completed by the end of the war, with a further four by the end of 1919. The completed aircraft were sent to No 9 (Newcastle) Aircraft Acceptance Park and from there moved to East Fortune in Scotland, the base of a torpedo-carrying squadron. En route, one of the aircraft crashed at Osset. The pilot, Lt.

H.L.Taylor, was unhurt. The remaining aircraft were delivered to London.

Meanwhile, the hangars and buildings of the RFC station at Doncaster were put up for sale. Two of the hangars were bought by Earl Fitzwilliam who had interests in the Sheffield car firm, Simplex. He planned to use them for car assembly and storage - but on a different site. Attempts were made to move the walls, but they failed. However, the roofs were dismantled and re-erected on a new industrial site on the road from Blaxton crossroads to Finningley village, just

Roof of the Belfast hangar originally   A. Childs
at the RFC station at Intake now part of a garage
at Finningley showing the intricate wooden roof support.

Roof of Belfast hangar at the Royal Air Force   After the Battle
Museum Hendon, the same type as the one now at Finningley. The aircraft
is a Wellington similar to the ones built by the Ministry of Aircraft
Production factory at Doncaster during the Second World War.

north of the level crossing. The roofs were of wood, a masterpiece of engineering, with a very complex system of wooden cross beams. Unfortunately, the occupants of the building nearer the railway found the wooden roof a fire hazard and had it replaced. The other hangar still has its original roof, and long may it remain.

So, two of the three hangars can be accounted for, even if one has had new walls and roof and the other only new walls. The fate of the third is rather sad. For over 50 years it remained on the original site, mainly as a bus garage, until in the seventies some one thought that this historic building stood in the way of progress and knocked it down. In its place a nice new modern monstrosity was built. Perhaps, given the chance, the same people might think that the Mansion House had served its time and replace it with a modern concrete box, a modern home for the Mayor of Doncaster.

With the departure of the Royal Flying Corps, now the Royal Air Force, Doncaster paused a little before succumbing to another bout of aviation fever. Doncaster race course was again the scene of the air circuses or air pageants, as they were variously known, provided by Alan Cobham and others. They were not on a particularly large scale but they certainly attracted large crowds - though not too many actually paid (shades of the 1909 display), it was too easy to get a free view. The arrival of these circuses was usually heralded by a formation fly-past over the town, rather in the way that ordinary circuses used to parade their animals before starting their shows. It was good publicity.

These pageants had a wide range of aircraft, including the forerunner of the helicopter, a C19 Autogiro, very advanced for its day. In one of these displays, in this case a Military Tattoo, a Vickers Virginia, possibly the largest and latest aircraft in the country, took off in the darkness from the race course, outlined for the occasion by hundreds of electric light bulbs.

There was other aircraft activity ... racehorse owners, jockeys and racegoers began to fly to Doncaster races, landing on the centre of the racecourse.

In 1920 the Government asked local authorities to assist in the formation of a chain of aerodromes so that this country would not lag behind other nations in the provision of civil air services. With the expert advice and encouragement of Alan Cobham, Doncaster set about its aim of making the town the Air Centre of the North and in 1931 they got parliamentary approval for a municipal airport on Low Pastures, across Bawtry Road from the racecourse. The approved site covered 126 acres with a planned extension to 414 acres. From time immemorial, Low Pastures had been used by freemen of the town to graze their cattle. The cottage of the neatherd, the man in charge of the grazing, was still there, but had been taken over by the Town Moor Golf Club as their clubhouse. It remained the clubhouse. By Act of Parliament, a 'right of way' across the site was extinguished to allow for proper development of the airport, but a bridge across the railway line on the east of the site to accommodate the right of way was retained and used later to join the two parts of the RAF camp that was to be established in the second world war.

In spite of all the efforts of the Doncaster Corporation, the first of Doncaster's new aerodromes was not to be at Low Pastures but at Armthorpe. On March 16, 1932, Danum Aero Club opened a small airfield on the eastern side of Hatfield Lane. It was little more than a large field with a small hangar in the far corner. However it served the club's purposes and when conditions were right, quite large aircraft could use the field. Opening day was marked by a six hour air display mounted by Alan Cobham, a generous gesture in view of his close connections with the developments at Doncaster.

Over the next couple of years, Armthorpe hosted a number of small club displays and gave many Doncastrians their first opportunity of a flight in a 'modern' aircraft. But there were several accidents, some of them caused by the smallness of the field. The first serious one was on August Bank Holiday, three months after the opening. At 8.30 in the evening, a Puss Moth took off with a pilot and two passengers. One was a 14 year old boy who had waited around most of the day, hoping for a chance of a flight. The pilot took pity on him and offered to take him up, but because of his size and age persuaded a spectator to go with them to make sure he didn't fall out. During the flight the aircraft stalled and crashed onto the airfield killing the two passengers and injuring the pilot. In the subsequent investigation, it was discovered that the pilot was not licensed for such a flight.

What was potentially a more sensational accident occurred in September 1933 when a De Havilland DH84 Dragon crashed on take-off into the woods on the other side of Hatfield Lane. The aircraft had been chartered to take racing people home after the St. Leger Meeting. Those on board included the jockey Gordon Richards, later Sir Gordon, and the trainer Fred Darling. Both escaped injury though the pilot Captain Pennington was killed. The investigation reported that the twin-engined aircraft failed to take off in a normal manner and ran nearly the full length of the aerodrome before it became airborne. It hit the boundary hedge and tipped over, nose-first, into the ground. It was concluded that the pilot had failed to open the throttle fully.

The Armthorpe field closed down soon afterwards - in 1934. Doncaster could now develop its newly prepared site on Low Pastures without local competition.

Avro Cadet at opening of Doncaster Airport 26th May 1936
Aircraft of this type also operated out of the airfield at Armthorpe
A.J.W. Smith

CHAPTER 2

1934-1939

Opening of Doncaster Airport on 26th May 1934 looking towards the Aeroplane
racecourse and the trees on the Great North Road. The aeroplanes belong to
Sir Alan Cobham who provided the opening display. The aircraft include a Handley Page Clive
airborne above flag poles and on the ground an Airspeed Ferry, DH Moth and DH Tiger Moth

Doncaster's planned aerodrome, grandly called 'aviation centre', was opened on May 26, 1934 by the Earl of Lonsdale. At a celebration lunch held in the Mansion House, Lord Lonsdale said that he hoped the enterprise would be as successful and beneficial to Doncaster as had been the coming of the railway works. Later in the day the Chairman of the Race Committee, the body responsible for the aerodrome, said that 'the first person, not a member of Doncaster Corporation, to speak about aviation, was Icarus'. Clearly, the Chairman was not fully informed of the fate of Icarus.

For the second time in two years, Alan Cobham (he became Sir Alan in October, 1926) provided the opening display for an aerodrome in Doncaster. There were no buildings to open, just 126 acres of level ground, with an entrance to Bawtry Road. The field was so level that one of the pilots taking part in the opening display said it was dangerous to fly upside down "because there were no bumps to help you judge your height". Facilities were sparse. Fire-fighting equipment was a thirty gallon foam extinguisher on a hand-cart operated by the entire staff of the airfield, a man called Edgar Needham. Fuel was brought over from a local garage by a small boy. The lack of toilet facilities was

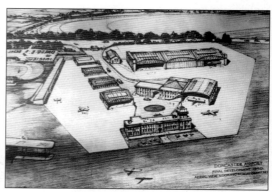

Optimistic artist's 1934 impression of W. Mills
Doncaster Airport in 1940.

enough to make Thomas Crapper, the Doncastrian who invented the water closet, turn in his sleep, but the Golf Club kindly made their facilities available. During the opening display, several competitions were held and the winners were given trophies first awarded in the 1909 display - they had been kept in safe custody by the Council (did they guess what was coming?).

The first race meeting after the airfield's opening was held a few days later on June 1 and 2. Several racegoers took advantage of the new aerodrome and came by air - a total of five aircraft landed on that occasion. Over the next 50 years, many of the top people in racing, including most, if not all, of the world's most famous jockeys, used the facilities. The twin peaks of traffic occurred just before and just after the second world war. At the 1938 St. Leger

Councillor G. H. Ranyard naming a DH 84 Dragon 'Spirit of Doncaster' before its first scheduled flight, and its last, to London   W. Mills

meeting, twenty or more aircraft, many of them small airliners, such as DH89 Rapides, brought hundreds of visitors.

On July 11, 1934, the aerodrome received its first non-racing VIP, the Prime Minister, Ramsey MacDonald. He was on his way from Scotland to Netherthorpe, Worksop, and arrived in a charted Aberdeen Airways DH84. He stopped at Doncaster to change planes. The aircraft that brought him to Doncaster crashed two days later, on Friday the 13th!

The first scheduled service to London - it was operated by Crilly Airways - opened on May 12, 1935. The aircraft used on the service, a DH84 Dragon, was officially named 'Spirit of Doncaster' by the Mayor just before the inaugural flight. Two people from the Doncaster area applied for season tickets. Other enquiries came from rugby supporters who wanted to know what arrangements had been made for trips to the forthcoming international between England and Ireland. Crilly hoped that the London service would be the first of many, with regular services to Birmingham, Bristol, Leicester, Norwich and Newcastle to be flown in partnership with Provincial Airways. Sadly these high hopes did not materialise and the Crilly Airways service to London operated only once and the company went into liquidation in 1936.

In 1935 the cost of landing at Doncaster was 1/- (one shilling - 5p) per aircraft plus 6d (sixpence - 2½p) per commercial passenger and 1/- per 500 lbs (four cubic feet) of freight, though it was agreed that RAF aircraft could land free of charge. Services at the aerodrome were improved. Fuel was available on site, though if an aircraft wanted an octane that the airport could not provide, a phone call was made to a local garage and it was sent over in two-gallon drums.

The first of the airport buildings was a hangar. It was built of reinforced concrete to a German design by J.H. Metcalf Bros of Doncaster. It could house twelve aircraft. The adjoining workshops were under the control of Captain W.A. Rollason of Rollason Aircraft Services. The Captain was also a director of Crilly Airways. Rollason's had their name painted over the hangar doors and 50 years later the name reappeared when the modern paint faded. (Another coincidence was that when the airfield was reopened 35 years later, one of the types of training aircraft used was the Rollason Condor built to a French design at Redhill in Surrey.)

Rollason Aircraft Services were given permission to operate pleasure flights, but those on Sundays were not allowed to fly over built up areas between 10.30 and 12.30 in the mornings and 6.00 to 8.00 in the evenings so as not to disrupt church services. These conditions were put in place because of the objections from the Superintendent Methodist Minister protesting at Sunday flying.

In April 1936 Captain Saint, an ex-Royal Naval Air Service pilot, was appointed Control Officer at a salary of £350 per year increasing by increments of £25 per year to a maximum of £400 per year. Captain Saint had just retired as chief test pilot of Gloster Aircraft Company and had the distinction of holding the first British 'B' Licence. Housing for the Control Officer and the Attendant were provided at a cost of £1,300 by building two houses on Bawtry Road by the airport entrance.

Aerial view of Doncaster Airport 1935. The white circle is 100 feet across.   W. Mills

1936 saw the continued development of the aerodrome with an application to be recognised as a 'customs airport'. Any previous mention of 'Doncaster Airport' was not strictly correct. An airport only becomes an airport when it possesses a customs station - which calls for special facilities. So, it was decided to build a control tower to give the customs officials the accommodation they needed and at the same time provide room for air traffic control. Walter Firth was contracted at a cost of £2,074 to build it. The ground floor contained a customs hall, offices for the passport inspectors, the Medical Officer of Health and the police, plus a booking office and weighing facilities, all in a space of about 50 feet by 20 feet. The customs officers had to be given two hours notice of any arrival, and the immigration officer was a member of the staff of a firm of solicitors in the town. On the first floor of the control tower, there was a wireless room and space for teleprinters. Meagre though these facilities might seem, it must be remembered that ten passengers would constitute a rush hour. The control tower was in direct teleprinter contact with Croydon and on from there to other airports in England and Europe. A second teleprinter was in contact with Manchester's airport at Barton (Ringway came later), which was the communications centre for the north of England. Doncaster was one of only four airports in Yorkshire to have a radio system and through it they were able to use the meteorological facilities at Barton.

It was hoped that an hotel would be built at the Bawtry Road entrance and, because of this, the Race Committee opposed an application to build another hotel further down the road. In the event, the other hotel, Punch's, was built, the airport hotel was not.

In 1936 discussions were held between the Airport Committee and the Air Ministry about the establishment of an Auxiliary Air Force (AAF) Unit. Land was acquired from the Jarratt estate to build housing and hangars for a permanent staff of three officers and about 50 other ranks as well as 24 auxiliary officers and 150 other ranks who were also auxiliaries. The unit would have 12 fighters and several training aircraft. It took the place of 503 (County of Lincoln) Squadron which was to be disbanded because of recruiting difficulties. Any members who wanted to transfer were welcome to do so. At the same time it was agreed that a Volunteer Reserve Unit could be formed at the airport.

Since the closure of the short-lived service to London by Crilly Airways, there had been no scheduled services through Doncaster. This state of affairs did not last for long. On July 1, 1936 the Dutch airline, KLM, in conjunction with British Continental Airways, altered their service from Amsterdam to Liverpool to call at Doncaster, partly in order to refuel. KLM had operated this service for two years, calling at Hedon near Hull, but the weather conditions at Hull were not satisfactory. After a careful inspection of Doncaster - which was approved - KLM substituted it for Hedon. To celebrate the occasion, the Corporation invited local worthies

Councillor Thomson, Chairman of the Aerodrome
Committee, handing the mail to the Mayor of Doncaster
T.H. Johnson, on the opening flight to Amsterdam. Mr de Vries of
KLM is on the right and Mr Ford, the creator of the airport and
Borough Surveyor is the third civilian from the right

W. Mills

to attend an event to mark the 'Inauguration of Continental Air Services' from Doncaster. The pioneering aircraft arrived from Liverpool at 12.20 pm. and left for Amsterdam at 12.35 with the Mayor and Mayoress of Doncaster, Councillor & Mrs. T.H. Johnson and the Town Clerk, Mr. W. Bagshaw and Mrs. Bagshaw among the passengers. After the plane had left, the guests were taken to the Mansion House for lunch where KLM officials complimented the Council and Mr. Ford, the Borough Surveyor, on the high standard of the airfield. Later the guests returned to the airport where they inspected the facilities. British Continental Airways then provided aircraft to give them flights over the town.

This first KLM flight from Doncaster was operated by a silver and blue tri-engined Fokker FX11 aircraft, registered PH-AID, piloted by Captain Hondong. The service was only scheduled to operate from July 1 to October 2 that year, restarting in the following spring.

The price of a return ticket to Liverpool was £2.5.0, single £1.5.0. A return to Amsterdam was £9, single £5. Flying time to Liverpool was 50 minutes, to Amsterdam under two hours. From Amsterdam there were onward connections to many other places on the Continent. One of the main reasons for the Amsterdam to Liverpool services was that if a person on the Continent wanted to travel to the United States,

KLM Fokker F X11 at Doncaster the inaugural
international service to Amsterdam after its arrival from
Liverpool on 1st July 1936.

C. E. Jackson

he would have to spend an extra two days travelling by sea as compared with flying to Liverpool and catching a boat from there. A number of the original passengers were people escaping the ever more serious political scene on the Continent, particularly in Nazi Germany.

LIVERPOOL - DONCASTER - AMSTERDAM

OPERATED BY BRITISH CONTINENTAL AIRWAYS.

in conjunction with Royal Dutch Air Lines (K.L.M.)

1 July to 3 October, Inclusive.

DAILY SERVICE, SUNDAYS EXCEPTED.

LIVERPOOL (Adelphi Hotel) ..	dep. 11.00	DONCASTER (Airport) ..	dep. 12.35
LIVERPOOL (Speke Airport) ..	dep. 11.40	AMSTERDAM (Schiphol Airp't)arr.	15.30
DONCASTER (Airport)	arr. 12.20	AMSTERDAM (Leidscheplein) arr.	16.05

N.B.—This service offers a connection with the K.L.M./A.B.A. service to Copenhagen and Malmo, leaving Amsterdam at 17.10.

AMSTERDAM - DONCASTER - LIVERPOOL

AMSTERDAM (Leidscheplein)	dep. 15.45	DONCASTER (Airport) ..	dep. 18.25
AMSTERDAM (Schiphol Airport) dep.	16.20	LIVERPOOL (Speke Airport) arr.	19.10
DONCASTER (Airport)	arr. 18.10	LIVERPOOL (Adelphi Hotel) arr.	19.50

N.B.—This service offers a connection at Amsterdam, for Doncaster and Liverpool, with the K.L.M./A.B.A. service from Stockholm, Malmo, and Copenhagen, arriving at 15.05.

Fares and Excess Baggage Rates

	Single Fare.	Return Fare. Valid 60 days	Excess Baggage Per Kg.
AMSTERDAM			
★ DONCASTER	Fls. 37.50	Fls. 67.50	Fls. 0.30
★ LIVERPOOL	Fls. 45.00	Fls. 81.00	Fls. 0.35
DONCASTER			
★ AMSTERDAM	£5 0 0	£9 0 0	9d.
★ LIVERPOOL	£1 5s. 0d.	£2 5s. 0d.	2d.
LIVERPOOL			
★ AMSTERDAM	£6 0s. 0d.	£10 16s. 0d.	11d.
★ DONCASTER	£1 5s. 0d.	£2 5s. 0d.	2d.

Timetable for the international service from Liverpool to Amsterdam with the fare list   G. Claybourn

In October 1936, the Mayor and the Chairman of the Airport Committee were present when the first airport lighting system was switched on. Chance Bros had installed floodlighting close to the control tower and the Cardiff Foundry and Engineering Co. had installed boundary lights. The Chance lighting was a complicated affair, a three lamp unit with three vertical shadow bars in front of the reflectors. Properly operated, a shadow could be formed so that the incoming pilot would not be dazzled. The boundary lights glowed, and the pilot would see a ring of red lights outside a sea of white light. During the day the boundary was marked by brightly painted boards.

Two Heyford night bombers from Finningley made a series of landings to inaugurate the new system. It was said the lighting was so powerful that Doncaster airport could be seen by pilots from the Pennines.

A company called North Eastern Airways was keen

Plan of Doncaster Airport 1936   G. Claybourn

Airspeed Envoy of North Eastern Airways at Doncaster 1938 employed on one of the local services. The aircraft half hidden on the left is possibly a DH Rapide W. Mills

to open night services and hoped to start experimental night flights between London and Scotland, calling at Doncaster. These night services were intended mainly to carry mail, though passengers would also be carried.

Further operations came to Doncaster when, in 1937, North Eastern Airways decided to make Doncaster an intermediate stop on their summer day-time service from Croydon to Perth and Aberdeen. They had previously called at Yeadon near Leeds, but the weather there had proved troublesome. On one of their flights, in October 1938, the airline carried the first airmail from Doncaster. The same airline, using Doncaster as a hub, also started services to Manchester and to Hull and Grimsby. They would also fly anyone who asked (and paid) from Hull to Grimsby or vice versa.

Among the airline directors was Lord Grimethorpe who was also connected with Airspeed, the firm that built the aircraft used in the services operating out of Doncaster. The first aircraft was the Airspeed Courier, powered by a single 240hp Armstrong Siddeley Lynx. It could carry up to six passengers at a top speed of 163mph. Another director was Nevil Shute Norway (better known as Nevil Shute the nov-elist). He actually started the company with Tillman, the chief designer. They

DH 89a Rapides of North Eastern Airlines in front of control tower 1937 C. E. Jackson

began work in an old bus garage in York and after building their first aircraft, an Airspeed Ferry, they moved to Portsmouth and built the Courier. Then followed a twin-engined version, the Airspeed Envoy, and it was these aircraft that became common sights in and over Doncaster. The Courier was one

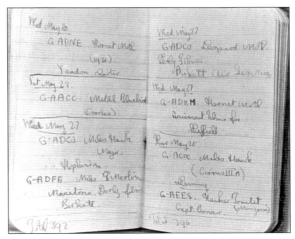

Notebook of young aircraft spotter Note Book for May 1936.
Note entry for 27th May when a Hornet Moth brought a
film for the Gaumont cinema then a regular service.

C. E. Jackson

of the first, if not <u>the</u> first, airliner to have retractable under-carriage. Later some of the services were taken over by the newer and larger Envoys.

The service was further upgraded when DH89s took over and the Couriers were confined to the local services to Hull and Grimsby, and the ferry service across the Humber. Manchester's Ringway airport was also joined to Doncaster by a scheduled service operated by a DH84.

Flying in those days had a genteel quality about it. A loaded aircraft possibly carried fewer than ten passengers and it was more likely than not that the pilot helped to load the passengers' luggage. If you lived in London and wished to fly to Doncaster, you simply telephoned Croydon Airport. A company car would pick you up at East Croydon station, on the Southern Railway, 20 minutes before the plane left and you had a personal escort to your aircraft. On arriving at Doncaster, you could

Doncaster Aero Club and visiting aircraft 1937 with Doncaster Rovers
football club in the background. Aircraft, left to right, Airspeed Courier,
BA Swallow, BA Pobjoy engined Swallow and BA Swallow.

STAR

choose between hiring a Steadman's taxi or walking to racecourse corner and catching a trackless trolleybus ('tracclus' to generations of Doncaster children). Return fare to Croydon was £4.5.0 against a first-class rail fare of £1.12.4. The first-class rail fare in the mid-nineties was £118. The equivalent airfare would be £350.

The expectation that Doncaster would become the 'aviation centre' of the North was based on what was then thought to be sound reasons. There were now up to 20 scheduled movements a day; the airport was within two miles of the main line station; and Doncaster was at the crossroads of an excellent (for the times) road system. Aircraft in the thirties had a very limited range and Doncaster was placed almost in the middle of the country.

Unfortunately, at least unfortunately for Doncaster, the development of airliners was such that intermediate stops such as Doncaster became unnecessary. But for a year or so, the number of scheduled air services calling at Doncaster was one of the highest in the North of England, although the only international service was to Amsterdam.

When the Borough Council planned the lay-out of the airport, provision had been made for the Doncaster Aero Club. A clubhouse had been built at the same time as the control tower and just behind it. The Club had previously been based in a caravan. The clubhouse had a bar, and there were regular dances and musical evenings. Members could use the hangar where they kept their aircraft for badminton. For all these facilities, the club paid a rent of £25 per year and a nominal fee for using the flying area.

Doncaster Aero Club

THIS CLUB is primarily a Club for those interested in active flying, but since there are some who, although interested in flying have no wish to take part in it as pilots, we have a scheme of Associate Membership at a reduced subscription.

No. of Members to date: 77.

Flying: 43.   *Associate:* 34.

Membership Rates are as follows:—

	Entrance Fee.	Subscription.
Flying Member	Nil.	£2-10-0
Associate Member	£1-1-0	£1- 0-0
Family Membership: One Member only per family	Nil.	10-0

FLYING RATES.

Dual Instruction	£1-15-0 per hour
Solo	£1-10-0 ,, ,,
Dual—10 hour Contract	£1-12-6 ,, ,,
Solo—10 hour Contract	£1- 7-6 ,, ,,

Why not take a TRIAL LESSON

10/6

and enjoy the thrill of having control of an aircraft

You will be made welcome if you get in touch with Mr. J. Hicklin, Chief Instructor, who will be pleased to show you over the Club premises and machines.

All instruction is carried out on D.H. Moth.

Part of the yearly handbook of Doncaster Aero Club showing cost of membership and flying rates 1937   G. Claybourn

Doncaster Aero Club had been formed by a group of local enthusiasts just after the airfield opened. The chief flying instructor was called Arthur Holland. When Arthur changed jobs and moved to the club at Netherthorpe aerodrome between Worksop and Sheffield, he was succeeded by E.W. (Jock) Bonar, a flier of some reputation - some years earlier he had flown in the Mildenhall-to-Melbourne air race.

By 1937 the club, now owned by Rollason Aircraft Services, had nearly 100 members. Flying members paid a yearly subscription of £2.10.0, associates paid £1.0.0. To begin with, it flew ex-RAF Avro 504s. It then acquired two British Aviation (BA) Swallows, a German training plane modified by BA, and several DH Puss Moth trainers. One of the club pupils who gained his licence with the club was Hughie Green, the famous entertainer.

Several private owners belonged to the club. Their aircraft, together with those belonging to the club and to visitors, plus the airliners making scheduled calls, made the airport a busy place.

The airport offered another unique service to the population of Doncaster whether they wanted it or not - aerial advertising. A company called Air Publicity trailed a banner behind the ubiquitous Avro 504N advertising anything anyone wanted them to advertise, provided they could afford it. A number of companies took advantage of the opportunity and the people of Doncaster were exposed to banners pointing out that 'Cephos cures headaches', and 'Bile Beans nightly keep you fit', as well as advising them to 'Enrol for National Service'. The exposure didn't last long. Aerial advertising was banned during the war and for several years afterwards.

Close to the airfield was Doncaster Rovers Football Club. A popular entertainment at half time, and at other times if play was not going well, was for the crowds packing the Rossington end to watch the flying. This habit continued during the war. How many German airfields gave our spies such a good view?

In 1937 it was agreed to build a second hangar to cater for the increased civilian traffic, particularly in light aircraft. Crouch and Sons of London were given the £4,500 contract. The hangar was to be built in reinforced concrete and with a barrel roof supported by a single space-saving concrete beam 100 foot long and 12 foot deep. The hangar was said to be bomb-proof. Attached to the side was a multi-coloured beacon which could be seen for miles. The beacon soon gained an unwanted reputation.

C. E. Jackson

Avro 504 Ns of Air Publicity Ltd., at Doncaster for aerial advertising of Co-op tea.

It flashed, in morse, the call sign for Doncaster (DC), but the mechanism was rather noisy. Every time the beacon flashed, there was a loud clump. It was the bane of nearby houses. It was said that pilots heard the beacon before they saw it.

KLM Lockheed 14, forerunner of the Lockheed Hudson, in a short stop over at Doncaster 1938. Beside the windsock on top of the tower is the D.J. Loop. C. E. Jackson

When the local residents in Belle Vue got to know about the proposed hangar, they objected but were overruled by the Council. However, it was agreed that brick cladding be used for the walls instead of concrete, at an extra cost of £61.

The facilities at the airport were now fairly comprehensive. With its hangars, radio communications, customs offices, meteorological services and night flying system, it rivalled any other airport in Yorkshire and possibly in the North. However, unknown to the Corporation's Airport Management, Doncaster's hopes of being a hub of scheduled services were doomed.

In 1937, KLM's partner, British Continental Airways, was taken over by British Airways, a forerunner of the present company, and withdrew from the service. British Continental Airways had used DH86s, a four-engined version of the DH Rapide. KLM, as the sole operator, phased out the smaller Fokker FX11 and introduced the more modern Douglas DC2, with an occasional DC3. These aircraft could easily fly nonstop from Amsterdam to Liverpool, with no need of intermediate refuelling. The stop at Doncaster became optional. Incidentally, the appearance of the DC3s began a connection with Doncaster that was to continue almost 60 years. The last DC3 to visit the airport did so a month before it finally closed on Christmas Day 1992.

Since the first in 1909, Doncaster had been the scene of regular displays, mainly on the racecourse and sometimes on Low Pastures. None of them had been on a large scale, but they had kept aviation interest in Doncaster alive. There were two displays (or pageants) in 1935 (the second celebrated the Silver Jubilee), one in 1936. Then there was one on every Empire Air Day for the next three years. Attendances varied from a few thousand to 25,000 in 1938, the biggest at the time in the country. The profits went to the Royal Air Force Benevolent fund.

The mainstay of these displays was the RAF, but civil aircraft were also involved, and there was stunt flying. In 1938 the aircraft taking part included the biplane fighters, Gloster Gauntlet and Gloster Gladiator, and the Hawker Hind, a biplane day bomber. The Vickers Wellesley also appeared - it was soon to capture the world distance record of 7,157 miles after 48 hours in the air - and there were bombers from Finningley and one of the first Hawker Hurricanes, the fighter that was to play such an important part in the Battle of Britain a couple of years later.

At the Empire Air Display in May 1937, an Airspeed Courier, a single engined airliner well known in the skies above Doncaster, took the place of a DH Rapide in giving pleasure flights. The pilot of the Rapide was Captain Jones who had already flown a number of such flights, each time finishing with a dive past the control tower at a height of 50 feet, followed by a climb and a half circuit before landing. At 7.20 Captain Jones took off in his Courier with five passengers. At the end of his flight he once again began to perform the usual dive past the control tower. This time the plane went into a roll, stayed upside down and went into a dive. Captain Jones tried to correct his attitude but did not have enough height and crashed to the east of the tower towards what was then Stotts Garage. Three of the five passengers were killed together with the Captain. One of the passengers was a teenager who had been helped into his seat by another passenger. His parents had watched the flight and the subsequent crash. Captain Jones was a well-known figure in the town. Before coming to Doncaster as depot manager and chief pilot of North Eastern Airways he had spent eight years in the RAF. He had then been an instructor at Brooklands.

It was the ambition of many companies to produce a cheap aircraft to enable the man in the street to become a pilot. One such scheme required people to build their own aircraft and Claybourn's Garage did just that.

Airspeed Courier after the crash at the Empire Air Display May 1937.   (Bruse/Leslie)

With plans provided by a Frenchman, Henry Miget, they built a small aircraft called the Pou-du-Ciel or, to non-French speakers, the Flying Flea, a single seater with a £45 30hp British Anzani engine. Because of a basic design fault, several Fleas failed to fly properly and crashed, with a number of fatalities. The aircraft eventually lost its Certificate of Air Worthiness. The Claybourn Flea was grounded and was used sometimes as part of a display in the car show room. After the second world war, it was loaned to the RAF and kept at Finningley. There an airman with a grudge against the RAF set fire to the hangar and destroyed several operational aircraft and the Flea, all told a loss of several million pounds. If this disgruntled airman had set fire to the hangar a few months earlier the outcome might well have been much more serious. The hangar had been used for Vulcans, a four-engined jet bomber designed to carry atomic bombs. The Flea was rebuilt by the RAF and, in September 1971, was formally presented to Graham Claybourn, son of the builder, by an RAF Air Vice Marshal. This aircraft is now on display at a museum at Breighton.

The Flea is not Claybourn's only claim to aviation fame. In the 1960s, Graham Claybourn decided that for a Christmas show in his garage he would have Santa come by plane. He borrowed a Tipsy Nipper (an aircraft of Belgian design and produced in kit form for people to build at home). The problem was how to get it from the airfield to his garage in Prince's St. It was rumoured, though Graham Claybourn now denies it, that he asked the police if he could land the aircraft in Waterdale during the night with the aid of the street lights and taxi it to his garage. The answer was to tow it through Bennetthorpe at the dead of night, much to the surprise of early Christmas revellers.

The airport had a continual stream of visitors in the years before the second world war. One of the more interesting was a German Flugkapitan, Hanna Reitsch, who flew in with a Klemm L32. This lady had gained world-wide renown by flying a Fokker-Wulf Achgelis, a twin rotor helicopter, indoors in front of Adolf Hitler. Some years later and in less happy times she helped in the test-flying of the prototype V1, the 'Doodlebug' flying bomb. This was not the only occasion that the swastika was seen at Doncaster. There were several visits by private aircraft from Germany on supposedly friendly tours of the country.

In February 1938 there was a major change in the management of the airport when the Air Ministry took over operational control. The Ministry controllers only worked during the day. Night flying was left in the hands of North Eastern Airlines, although the Air Ministry Wireless/Telegraph operators remained on duty.

In 1938 there was another Air Ministry scheme whereby anyone who wanted to learn how to fly could join the Air Guard. The Air Ministry paid half the fees. A unit was set up at Doncaster, but it was not a complete success.

As war in Europe became increasingly likely, the threat of bombing was taken more seriously. The Air Ministry intensified the training of the country's anti-aircraft defences and as part of this training North Eastern Airways won a contract to provide aircraft for army co-operation duties. This involved flying set patterns at night for the training of searchlight and anti-aircraft batteries in detection and range-finding. No-one actually fired a gun. North Eastern Airways had a fleet of around six DH89s. The contract was a salvation to them and other companies that took part in the exercises.

Mixture of DH84 Dragons, DH89a Rapides and DH 90 Dragonflys belonging or on hire to North Eastern Airways for army co-operation duties 1939. Note Chance Light in front of hangar. W. Mills

On November 1, 1938, the long-planned Auxiliary Air Force (AAF) Squadron was formed. It was called 616 (South Yorkshire) with a Yorkshire rose as its badge and *Nulla rosa sine spina* (No rose without a thorn) as its motto. Its initial equipment was six Hawker Hind day bombers, two Tutor trainers and two Avro 504s, a throw-back to the first world war. The squadron was initially part of Bomber Command. However on November 15, it was transferred to Fighter Command and re-equipped with its fighters, Gloster Gauntlets, the last open cockpit fighters in the RAF and placed under the command of Squadron Leader, the Earl of Lincoln. During the summer more aircraft arrived, Tutors, four Fairey Battles and the occasional Hurricane - the last two types giving the squadron experience on modern monoplanes.

The squadron had a nucleus of full-time members of the RAF but its main task was to train part-timers. The AAF Squadrons were not simply a reserve to support the RAF in time of war. They were fully-fledged permanent additions to Britain's air strength.

Hawker Hind of 616 (South Yorkshire) Squadron at Doncaster 1938. STAR

Gloster Gauntlets of 616 (South Yorkshire) Squadron at Doncaster 1938. Graham Pitchfork

From its inception, the AAF's dominating inspiration was 'esprit de corps' and a fiercely guarded pride of identity. Deliberate flouting of regular RAF customs was paramount among its highly individualistic members, as witnessed by 601 Squadron's habit of wearing red socks with uniform. The same squadron regularly displayed a notice at annual camps, "AAF ONLY - tradesmen and RAF etc use entrance at rear". They had the privilege of belonging to a first-class club but instead of paying an entrance fee, they themselves were paid, and paid for doing what they liked best, flying. But any debt they might have to the country was soon to be repaid many times over, often with their lives.

Pilots, though trained by RAF instructors to a very high standard, sometimes had the odd problem. For example, on one occasion when one of the instructors and a student took off in

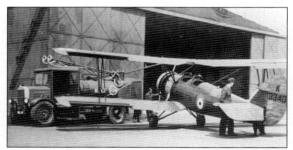

Avro Tutor of 616 of (South Yorkshire) Squadron with Albion refuelling tender at Doncaster 1939. Graham Pitchfork

a Hind, the wires of the controls had been connected the wrong way round. As the aircraft took off it suddenly reared up and fell back onto its tail, turning over and catching fire. Both occupants walked away unhurt.

Every year 616 Squadron had a summer camp. In 1939, it went to Manston, Kent. One of the pilots was Acting Pilot Office (A/PO) 'Cocky' Dundas who later became one of our most famous fighter aces - though not the <u>most</u> famous. That claim could best be made by Group Captain Douglas Bader, whose step-father was the vicar at Sprotborough, near Doncaster. He achieved his fame despite losing both his legs in a flying accident. He became a Wing Commander and leader of the Tangmere wing (which included 616 Squadron) before being shot down over France

Group Captain J. Glover in 1938 was member of 616 (South Yorkshire) Squadron and later commanded 271 Squadron.   J. Glover

Buck Casson one of the original members of 616 (SouthYorkshire) Squadron. He was shot down in August 1941 over France in the same operation as Group Captain Douglas Bader   Buck Casson

in early August 1941. Shot down in the same operation, within a few minutes of Bader, was Buck Casson, a Sheffield man, who had joined 616 Squadron in those happy carefree days at Doncaster.

Hawker Hind after crash at Doncaster 1938   Graham Pitchfork

Avro Tutors and a Fairey Battle of 616 (South Yorkshire) Squadron on summer camp at Manston August 1939.   Graham Pitchfork

On August 23, while still at their summer camp at Manston, the squadron, together with all other auxiliary squadrons, was embodied into the RAF. They were given the news at a special parade. All personnel were conscripted into the RAF and

New recruits for 616 (South Yorkshire) Squadron arriving at Ellers Road for RAF Doncaster on the outbreak of war 1939.

Graham Pitchfork

ordered to report forthwith to Doncaster Airport. The ground staff were confined to camp and a couple of days later they were put on a train for an unknown destination. They ended their mystery tour at St. James sidings, Doncaster, to find a fleet of Corporation buses waiting to take them to the airfield. Once there they were again confined to camp for a further five days. They were then allowed to send a telegram to inform their families that they had returned to Doncaster and to ask them to fetch their civilian clothes. Ironically, almost all the squadron's personnel lived close by, some even in Bessacarr. It would have been quicker for them to walk home to tell their families where they were. However, any officer with a car had been permitted to make his own way from Manston to Doncaster.

Form 1445D
(Pads of 50)

Ref No. 108

AUXILIARY AIR FORCE

NOTICE OF CALLING OUT

under the

Reserve and Auxiliary Forces Act, 1939

Name   RADCLIFFE . A.

Rank   A.C.2.   Number 814196   Unit 616 (SY) Squadron

Following Directions given by the Secretary of State in accordance with an Order by His Majesty in Council, made under Section 1 (1) of the above-mentioned Act, you are as a member of the Auxiliary Air Force called out for service during the period——————— to——————— both dates inclusive.

You are hereby required to attend at Doncaster Airport not later than——————— o'clock on the first date above mentioned. Should you not present yourself as ordered you will be liable to be proceeded against.

Date 23/8/39

Clowe
Adjutant

Unit 616 (SY) Squadron
Auxiliary Air Force

INSURANCE CARDS AND UNEMPLOYMENT BOOKS.
If you are subject to the National Health Insurance and Unemployment Insurance Acts, you are required to bring your card and book with you when joining.

(5831) Wt. 17302—1000 5,000 Pads 6/39 T.S. 700

Notice of Calling Out for AC2 A. Ratcliffe
11 days before declaration of war

A. Ratcliffe

CHAPTER 3
1939-1945

The war came two days early to Doncaster. On September 1, 1939, the airport was requisitioned by the Air Ministry and placed under the command of Squadron Leader, the Earl of Lincoln, squadron commander of 616 (South Yorkshire) Squadron. A small point: Doncaster Airport had ceased to be an airport and reverted to being an airfield - it had lost its customs post!

When war did start, No 7 Squadron Bomber Command arrived from Finningley equipped with eight Hampden bombers and eight Anson trainers. Its task at Doncaster was to train its crews to the standard of 5 Group Bomber Command. Unfortunately on September 5, Pilot Officer A.R. Playfair was killed while flying a training mission in a Hampden bomber. His plane crashed into Cockwood Farm, Cantley. He was buried at Finningley Parish Church. Over five years later, in November 1944, another aircraft, a Halifax, crashed on the same farm. It had just taken off from nearby Lindholme. This time the crew survived.

The squadron returned to Finningley after three weeks at Doncaster but not before another Hampden had crashed near Red House Farm on the racecourse, this time again without casualties. A week later the squadron moved again to Upper Heyford and in October, 1940 was transferred to No 8 Group under Air Vice Marshal D.C.T. Bennett, based at Oakington. It became part of the Pathfinder Force that led Bomber Command units on attacks on enemy territory.

616 (South Yorkshire) Squadron officers at Doncaster 1939.   Graham Pitchfork
Left rear: Smith, Dundas. Rear: Bell, Grimshaw, Holden, Wilson, Wood, Moberley, Osborne.
Centre: Winn, Kellet, Lord Lincoln (CO), Glover, Hatchwell, Brewster, Casson, Roberts.
Front: Hellyer, St. Aubyn, Murray, Graydon.

616 Squadron's stay at Doncaster was also short-lived. On October 23, it moved to Leconfield, near Beverley in east Yorkshire where it re-equipped with Spitfires. It went on to play an honourable part in the Battle

The two areas circled on bottom right of map are enlarged and displayed on following pages

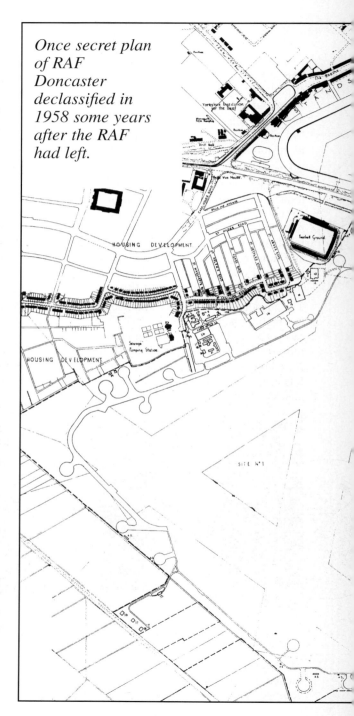

Once secret plan of RAF Doncaster declassified in 1958 some years after the RAF had left.

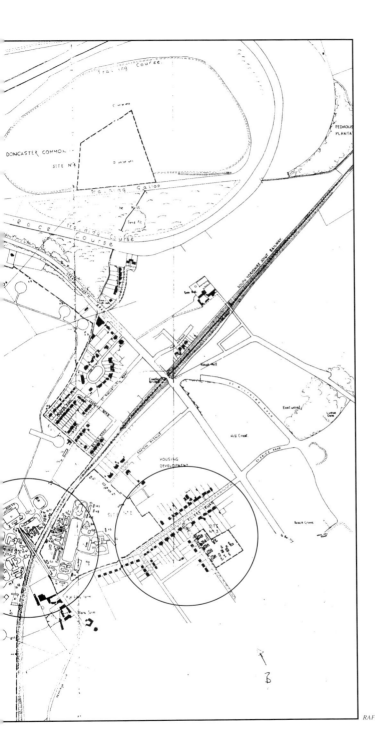

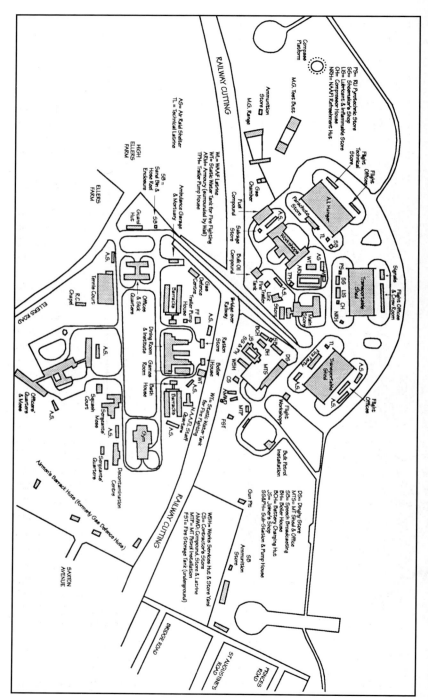

PS= RU Pyrotechnic Store
SS= Shoemaker's Shop
LS= Lubricant & Inflammable Store
CH= Compressor House
NRH= NAAFI Refreshment Hut.

Compass Platform

RAILWAY CUTTING

M.G. Test Butts

Ammunition Store
M.G. Range

Flight Technical Store

Flight Offices

A.I. Hangar

Gas Chamber

Fuel Compound

Pyrotechnic Store

Workshops

AS
TL
SB

WT
ARK
TPH

WSH
Main Store

Signals
Flight Offices & Crew Room

Transportable Shed

PS SS LS CH
NRH

Transportable Shed

Flight Offices

AS

Flight Workshops

AS

Bulk Petrol Installation

Gun Pit

SB Ammunition Store

DS= Dinghy Store
MTS= MT Shed & Office
SBs= Speech Broadcasting
BH= Boiler House
BCH= Battery Charging Hut
JS= Joiner's Shop
SS&PH= Sub-Station & Pump House

WSH= Works Services Hut & Store Yard
CS= Contractor's Store
AMMO= Ammo. Compound, Store & Latrine
MTP= MT Petrol Installation
FST= Fire Storage Tank (underground)

RAILWAY CUTTING

SAXON AVENUE

Armont's Barrack Huts (formerly Gas Defence Huts)

BRIDGE ROAD

ST. AUGUSTINE'S ROAD

PRINCES ROAD

Decontamination Centre

Sergeants' Quarters

Sergeants' Mess

Officers' Quarters & Mess

AS

Gym

NAAFI Staff Quarters

Barracks

WT

Bath House

Games House

Dining Room & Institute Room

Boiler House

Ration Store

Offices & Sick Quarters

Barracks

Gas Defence Centre

Trailer Pump House

FF
AS

DS
JS PH
SBs BH
BCH
MTS

F&T

AMMO

MTP

WT= Static Water Tank for Fire Fighting

Tennis Court
R.C. Chapel

AS
Guard Hut
SB

Ambulance Garage & Mortuary

Sludge Store

Bulk Oil Compound

Fire Tank

Link Trailer

AS

Transportable Shed

7L
SB

Signals

Bridge over Railway

HIGH ELLERS FARM

ELLERS FARM

ELLERS ROAD

WA= WAAF Latrine
WT= Static Water Tank for Fire Fighting
ARK= Armoury (surrounded by Wall)
TPH= Trailer Pump House

AS= Air Raid Shelter
TL = Technical Latrine

SB = Sand Bin & Hose Reel Enclosure

Ammunition Store

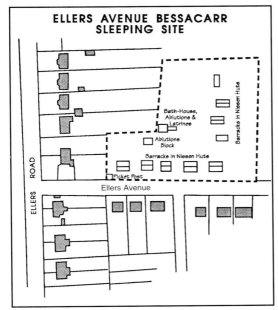

ELLERS AVENUE BESSACARR SLEEPING SITE

Barracks In Nissen Hute

Bath-House, Ablutions & Latrines

Ablutions Block

Barracks In Nissen Huts

Picket Post

Ellers Avenue

ELLERS ROAD

of Britain and saw much service throughout the rest of the war. It was the first squadron to be equipped with Meteors, the first allied jet fighter. The squadron was disbanded at Worksop on March 3, 1957.

Not all the squadron had gone to Leconfield. 50 men whose training had not been completed stayed behind for a couple of months before rejoining their colleagues. The airfield at Doncaster now had no home-based squadrons and was reduced to a care and maintenance basis with only a skeleton staff under the command of P/0 Grodon. It was used as a dispersal site mainly for Hampden aircraft from 61 and 144 bomber squadrons based at Hemswell, half of each squadron arriving in the afternoon and departing the next morning. One of the Hampdens crashed onto the airfield, ammunition exploding, but without casualties.

Before the war, the emergency services had been few and far between - a case of one man and his dog - except in the case of Doncaster there was no dog. This state of affairs could not continue on an operational RAF station and additional equipment was borrowed from Finningley. Troops from the 57th regiment Royal Artillery arrived to take over guard duties and they were later replaced by men from the West Yorkshire regiment.

Three years earlier, negotiations had been held between the Local Authority and C.W. Aviation, on behalf of the Air Ministry, about the possibility of building an aircraft factory on the north side of the airport. These talks had broken down (the Airport Committee would not release the site the Air Ministry wanted nor did they like the design) but by the outbreak of war the problems had been overcome and Westland Aircraft Co of Yeovil had formed a company, Westland (Doncaster) Ltd, to build and manage a factory for the Ministry of Aircraft Production. Assembly of the prefabricated building began shortly after the beginning of the war, but it was not until late 1940 that it came into production. The Air Ministry had placed an order for 500 Lysander reconnaissance aircraft. Until the new factory was ready, some construction work was carried out in one of the pre-war hangars.

The factory was built on the site originally proposed and anyone who remembers it will sympathise with the hesitations of the Airport Committee. Even the camouflage paint could not hide its ugliness and the people in St. Cecilia's Road, Belle Vue, must have rued the day when it was built. It completely blocked out the view from their rear gardens.

While there was little aerial activity, building on the airfield went on apace. The defences had been upgraded by the construction of a number of pill boxes with their own internal telephone system and armed with Lewis guns. Many of the buildings had been camouflaged - even the bomb-proof hangar had its yellow paint covered over - and the control tower had a blast wall built around it. (Thirty or so years later when the wall was to be taken down, everyone thought it was going to be an easy job. The company then managing the airfield organised a Sunday treat. Volunteers were armed with sledge hammers, children brought skipping ropes and picnic baskets and attempts were made to knock the wall down. After an all-day assault they had to give in. Hardly a splinter had come away. They knew how to build blast walls in those war-time days! Modern science, in the form of a huge bulldozer, finally did the trick in a couple of hours.)

The Air Ministry was concerned that the airfield was still not camouflaged enough and sent a couple of experts to see what further should be done. After a good look round they decided that the racecourse would always give the game away - how could you camouflage a racecourse? The solution was to build a prisoner of war camp on the racecourse's Silver Enclosure.

Meanwhile, construction of accommodation billets at the airport for several hundred RAF men and WAAF women went vigorously ahead and the accommodation already built for 616 (South Yorkshire) Squadron was taken over and extended. These developments took place on the Bessacarr side with entrance from Ellers Road. The domestic site was on the Bessacarr side of the railway line together with quarters for officers and men, not forgetting the much loved parade ground and guard house. Over the railway bridge was the technical site with the three hangars - in official language, one RAF type Al hangar and two transportable sheds. These were in addition to the Bellman hangar at the bottom of Sandy Lane, a gas chamber (for testing gas-masks), firing ranges, ammunition stores and all the other services needed to equip an operational squadron. Even more accommodation was required and some open space was taken over in Ellers Avenue, now the site of an infants school. 16 barrack blocks, enough for several hundred men, were built. The driveway can still be seen today.

Even all this accommodation was not enough and private houses and other buildings were requisitioned, including 28 Bawtry Road which provided space for 30 airmen and their tents, Whitegates in St. Eric's Road for another 30 airmen and two NCOs, and other houses in Saxton Avenue. Also taken over was the old Tote offices behind the Wheatley Hotel, and Eastfield house on Grandstand Road, now Leger Way, then part of the Deaf School. Other officers were billeted in private houses around the Ellers Road area. WAAFs were billeted in a large house on Thorne Road - a lorry picked them up each morning, as it did those WAAFs who lived at home. How kind of the RAF to provide a taxi service! Trees bordering the airport on Bawtry Road were chopped down to clear the approach to one of the runways. Even the street lamps were reduced in height.

It was the time of the phoney war, but the airport was taking no risks.

Exercises were held to practise defending it. On occasions troops from outside Doncaster played the part of the attacking force and often the Home Guard helped the defenders. Gas attacks, one of the main fears at the time, were simulated. The result, given by the umpires, always seemed to favour the defending side. The exercise normally ended with just enough time for a pint.

Two outstations were built, the first in the centre of the racecourse. This was a HF/DF (High Frequency/Direction Finding) facility which enabled some direction guidance be given to aircraft at night and in bad weather. It also helped combat the industrial haze which often covered the airfield. The second installation was at Cantley, near where the two water towers are today. This was the highest land near to the airfield and the most suitable site for a transmitting station. The control tower at the airfield was only just above sea level which would limit the reach of transmitters. A rifle range had been established in Cantley, near the cemetery, firing towards the railway.

On October 29, 1939 a number of civilian aircraft arrived, including two Ensigns, a DH86, a Fokker Trimotor and two Handley Page (HP) 42s, all manned by civilian crews from Imperial Airways, British Airways and

Bristol Bombay possibly at Doncaster 1940

Handley Page Harrow possibly at Doncaster 1940. RAFM

Jersey Airways. These aircraft were operated by the Civil Aircraft Flight under the command of the National Air Communications Unit of Fighter Command. They were incorporated into 1680 Flight and used on communication duties. As they were manned by civilians they could not normally be operated as military aircraft, so their usefulness was limited.

As a sign that things were about to change, the command of the station was upgraded when Flight Lieutenant Wynyard-Wright was posted in from Debden as the new Station Commander. Early in 1940, two Squadron Leaders arrived to inspect the station and assess the possibility of it operating a yet-to-be-formed squadron. The answer must have been favourable because with a few weeks a new squadron, 271, was formed.

It was not the first 271 Squadron. In September 1918, a squadron with the same number was formed at Otrano in Southern Italy, equipped with Felixstowe seaplanes. Its task was to prevent Austro-Hungarian submarines from leaving the Adriatic. This requirement was short-lived and the squadron was disbanded within a few months.

The authority for the formation of 271 Squadron came in a secret document prepared by Group Captain L.N.Hollinghurst and issued by the Air Ministry on March 2, 1940. It read:

Handley Page Sparrow, a conversion of the Harrow. RAFM

Formation of No 271 (Transport) Squadron

The above squadron will form at Doncaster on March 8, 1940. It will be in 12 Group Fighter Command.

2. This squadron will take over certain responsibilities hitherto borne by the National Air Communications (NAC). Inter alia it will be responsible for:

(i) Air transport required in connection with the move of bomber or fighter squadrons within the United Kingdom or from the United Kingdom to France.

(ii) Air transport required in connection with moves between Flying Training Schools and Bombing or Gunnery Schools (for armament training).

3. As an interim measure, NAC will provide civil aircraft to maintain the equivalent of 271 Squadron on a civil basis as from March 8, 1940. This will continue until such a time as the hand-over of NAC aircraft is completed and 271 Squadron is formed on a service basis.

4. The aircraft establishment to commence with will be: one Bombay, two HP42s, two Scyllas, one Fokker 12, one Ford Trimotor and three Harrows.

5. In addition to the above, 10 DH Rapides and 10 DH Dragons on the establishment of No 110 AAC Wing will be annotated to the Air Transport Squadron should circumstances necessitate it. These Dragons and Rapides will normally be employed by No 100 Wing in providing anti-aircraft cooperation.

6. The squadron will be service-manned although it is possible that a proportion of the pilots, and possible maintenance personnel, will be provided by enlistments of personnel hitherto employed by NAC.

7. The Air Transport Squadron will normally be used to carry out duties which are within the province of No 24 Squadron.

8. Demands for the services of this Air Transport Squadron should be made to Air Ministry (E11) who will be the controlling authority subject to any overriding limitations on the use of aircraft which may be imposed from time by DDWO.

Thus was 271 Squadron conceived - though the HP42s and Scyllas specified were missing.

The new squadron, motto 'Death and Life' with a badge of a gauntlet holding a cross, was formed on March 28, but only began referring to itself as 271 Squadron on May 1 when the squadron's official documents began. Wing Commander Millen arrived on April 6 to assume command of the new squadron and the station. On April 27 the squadron was transferred to Bomber Command.

The first aircraft to be delivered to the new squadron was a Ford Trimotor, not to be confused with the Fokker Trimotor. It was a development of the plane flown by Commander Byrd in the first flight over the South Pole. It was built by the Ford Motor Company using the mass-production techniques they had pioneered for the manufacture of cars. It had belonged to the Hon. A.E.Guinness and had been impressed into the RAF. It took part in a number of the early flights of the squadron to France but on September 1, 1940, it flew to Northern Ireland and because of heavy rain was forced to land on the shore of Belfast Lough. It overshot the small field and ended in a ditch and although the damage was slight it was struck off the strength of the squadron.

The first Bombay aircraft for the squadron were collected on May 3 from Kinloss on the Moray Firth on the north-east coast of Scotland. The Bombay was a fairly large twin-engined aircraft built by Bristol to meet an Air Ministry requirement issued in the early 1930s for a night bomber and transporter. The first models were built in a new factory in Belfast. The aircraft was powered by two Bristol Pegasus Xll engines and its bomb load was carried internally. It also had rotatable gun turrets in both the nose and tail. With a take off and landing run of about 500/600 yards, it fitted well into Doncaster. However the aircraft was obsolete, as a bomber, even when it was being built. The newer Hampdens, Whitleys and Wellingtons had taken over their proposed bomber role and Bombays were relegated to their secondary duty, as troop and freight carriers. It was in this role, and without their guns, that they came to Doncaster. They were followed soon afterwards by the Handley Page Harrow, a similar aircraft to the Bombay, but slightly larger. Like the Bombay it was not up to the standard of the newer bombers. It too reverted to its secondary role, again without its guns.

Shortly after their arrival, one of the Harrows was sent to Tollerton in Nottinghamshire to be further modified. The guns had already been removed and in the modification, the three turrets were also removed, as was the bomb bay. This enabled the floor to be lowered a foot or so and the saving in space and weight allowed up to 32 passengers to be carried.

Savoia-Marchetti SM73P possibly at Doncaster.   RAFM

The modification was a success and over the next months, all the squadron's Harrows were modified and the modified aircraft were called, unofficially, Sparrows.

On May 10, 1940 Germany invaded the

Low Countries and the phoney war was over. The same day 271 Squadron's first operational sortie took place - and the first set-back. Bombays and the Ford Trimotor went to Betheniville in France taking supplies to 501 squadron. One of the aircraft crashed on landing, killing three of its passengers and injuring every one else, one of the crew seriously. Two days later, another Bombay got into trouble and had to jettison its load. It was thought that both incidents were linked and that their cargoes had been improperly stowed. It must be remembered that although the aircraft had been in service for some time as bombers, there was little experience of using them as troop and freight carriers. It was a very sobering start to the squadron's real war.

On a trip to Amiens, a Harrow had been damaged on landing and the Ford Trimotor was sent over with a spare part. It was too big to be carried internally and had to be strapped to the undercarriage.

Back at Doncaster, while the momentous events were taking place 300 miles or so away, the station staff found time to 'Dig for Victory' and two acres of the airfield disappeared under vegetables. Word did however get through that something was afoot in far-off places and all leave was cancelled and those on leave recalled. 20 men of the 5th Battalion South Staffordshire Regiment were sent for to help defend the station. They mounted guard for four hours a day, two hours in the morning, two in the afternoon. If the enemy came at any other time, they would have to wait.

Further additions to the squadron strength came with the fall of Belgium. Four Savoia-Marchetti SM 73P, three-engined 18 seater passenger aircraft of Italian manufacture belonging to Sabena Airlines, the Belgian national airline were put into service, often using crews of different nationalities. Their time at Doncaster was short but violent. On May 22, a Savoia-Marchetti piloted by Pilot officer McClaren was posted missing over France. Thankfully he had landed safely, but worse was to follow two days later. A mixed formation of transport aircraft, including civilian aircraft operated by civilian crews, took food and ammunition to Merville in France. They were attacked while on the ground by German fighters and one of the aircraft was destroyed. On the way home, they were fired on by anti-aircraft guns and one of the Savoia-Marchettis crashed. At the end of the month the remaining aircraft were returned to Sabena who used them on their African routes.

When war broke out, the RAF did not have any heavy transport squadrons at home, though there were some in the Middle East. The only transport they did have was 24 Squadron based at Hendon but this flew smaller aircraft and used them to transport VIPs. With the formation of 271 Squadron, the Hendon aircraft continued to be used for the lighter work and 271 Squadron undertook the heavier duties. But with the growing need to move men and supplies to and from France, several of Doncaster's aircraft were detached to Hendon to join 24 Squadron. From

Hendon and Croydon these aircraft ferried personnel and supplies of all kinds to both the British Expeditionary Force (BEF) and to RAF squadrons. A number of the first flights were to Le Havre carrying barrage balloons. On one occasion, an aircraft was forced to land at Deauville and needed customs clearance from the French before being allowed to proceed. There might be a war on and we might be friends, but 'Rules is Rules' and you have to get customs clearance first. It seems that in parts of France the phoney war still existed.

The squadron was also called upon to take Government officials and documents to Paris. But as the Germans advanced, the squadron had to give more and more help to the badly battered RAF squadrons, ferrying replacement crews to France and bringing back non-essential personnel. Supplies were still carried for the BEF.

These old Harrows carried up to two tons of freight and could operate out of small fields - a better performance than the Douglas Dakotas which would replace them in three years time.

However at the end of May, replacements arrived in the form of three Handley Page 42s - the Hannibals. These majestic aircraft had been the flagships of Imperial Airways, entering service on July 11, 1931 on the Paris route. The Hannibal was a biplane powered by four 525hp Bristol Jupiter engines, able to carry 38 passengers on European services and 18 on longer routes. It was said that if you had time and money to spare you could fly in great comfort and be treated like a Lord at a little over 100mph. In 1932 they started services to South Africa, flying via Cairo, travelling only by day with passengers spending the night at four-star hotels on the ground. The journey took around four days, if there were no hold-ups - still rather faster that the six weeks or more by boat. In this way, they brought the Empire closer together. These genial giants provided a level of comfort unrivalled by any other land plane and were much appreciated by the Kings, Queens, potentates and the like they were accustomed to carrying. Now they were press-ganged into carrying Airman Jones and Private Smith and boxes of oily spare parts. What a come-down! However, because of their slow speed and the sedate way they progressed through the air, they rarely operated over France. They would have stood little chance against German fighters.

The situation in France had grown desperate. The evacuation from Dunkirk was into its second week and 271 Squadron was now helping to withdraw as many personnel as possible - and their equipment. It was also used to evacuate personnel from central and southern France, using Jersey to refuel - and sometimes just avoiding the advancing Germans.

An account of one of these trips was given by an airman fitter AC1 John MacDonald (Harrows and Bombays carried a fitter and a rigger as part of the aircrew). AC1 MacDonald was based at Doncaster. Here is his account of one of those flights.

A Day in the life of 271 Squadron

"I have been asked to relate the story of what happened to a Handley Page Harrow flight to France, about a month after Dunkirk.

The rigger ACl Dale (a Canadian) and myself were ordered to get our machine ready for flight. Eventually the two pilots appeared - Flight Lieutenant Glover and a Sergeant Pilot, a Canadian, whose name I cannot recall. Flight Lieutenant Glover took the controls and began to taxi out for take off. After about 200 yards, he complained to the rigger that the rudder bar was a bit sluggish. However after a while he seemed to be satisfied and the plane was ready for take off.

The first leg was to Jersey for fuel and confirmation for the rest of the journey to Nantes. We all expected the second leg to be called off but when Flight Lieutenant Glover came out of the flight office he said "We carry on". We took off for Nantes. The flights in those old Harrows could be very boring so to relieve the monotony I went aft to look out of the central turret. As soon as I looked at the tail unit I realised why the controls were a bit sluggish. One of the fins was hanging to one side at an angle of about 45°! I informed the pilots. Flight Lieutenant Glover said there was nothing we could do at this stage except carry on and land without doing a circuit of the drome. As we approached for the landing, we all realised the airfield had been made unlandable, as it were, with obstacles placed in such a position that aircraft could not land without colliding with one or more of them. With very good handling, Flight Lieutenant Glover brought her down beautifully but could not avoid hitting one of the objects near the end of the run in - but the only damage was a bent radius rod.

The reason we had been sent to Nantes was to bring back the last of 98 Squadron's officers and documents (Nantes was the squadron's base for 98 Squadron and its Fairy Battles. It was my old squadron before 271). With the demise of the Harrow, there were four more for repatriation. Flight Lieutenant Glover went to the flight office to find out the next move.

He came back about an hour later with the information that another plane had been sent for but would not arrive until the following morning. In the meantime we were told to fill the tank of one of the vans with petrol (there were dozens of vehicles, motor cycles etc left behind). We also filled as many cans as the van could carry. If Jerry came during the night we were to make for St. Nazaire and try to get a passage to UK. We slept in the van that night (my breath smelt of petrol for months). About 3.30 next morning we heard the drone of an aircraft approaching. To our relief, it was an Albatross freighter. The pilot landed but didn't even switch the engines off. We scrambled aboard and headed for Blighty, smartish."

Boulton Paul Defiant which suffered so badly at the hands of the German fighters. G. H. Oakes

By a kind twist of fate, the pilot of the Harrow in MacDonald's flight to Nantes, Flight Lieutenant, now Group Captain, Glover, is still alive and well and living in North Cornwall. His memory of the incident differs somewhat from that of AC1 MacDonald - not surprisingly since it took place over 50 years ago. He remembers that the Harrow was not unairworthy but was burnt at Nantes. They returned to England in a HP42 of 271 Squadron, not an Albatross and the ship they intended to catch if no plane arrived to pick them up had been bombed and set on fire - he had seen it burning. They did not intend to use a van. Instead, they had taken the car left by the Station Commander and filled <u>that</u> with petrol. The plan was to make for Spain. He thought they would have made it, but in fact they had no need to try.

John Glover had joined the RAF in the early 1930s. In 1938 he was an instructor with 616 Squadron and moved with them to Leconfield. He stayed with the squadron for a few weeks, but the work did not make use of his training. He filled in time by giving instruction in night-flying. He then contracted jaundice which took him temporarily off flying duties. After a time with the Air Ministry in London and a number of other temporary jobs, he wanted to get back to flying. In the end he was sent to the Central School of Gunnery - he knew nothing about gunnery. One night when he was station duty officer, a signal came from the Air Ministry asking for volunteers to go to Norway as bomber/transport pilots. He was a fully-trained bomber/transport pilot with experience in the Middle East, so he sent a signal offering himself and giving his details. He was posted the following day to a squadron being formed to go to Norway, but by then the Germans had occupied the whole country. The base of the squadron was at Doncaster with various aircraft. 271 Squadron stayed and John was back at Doncaster in time to take the flight to Nantes.

The entry in the squadron diary for June 18 says that an aircraft from Doncaster was instructed by a senior officer to leave Istres, Southern France, as soon as possible and head home the fastest way. One of the pilots concerned was Cresswell Viney. Remarkably he is able to give an eyewitness account of the sortie and how, before this flight, he came to Doncaster.

Cresswell Viney joined the Volunteer Reserve (the RAF's equivalent to the army's Territorials and the Royal Navy's Naval Reserve) in 1937 and was taught to fly at Filton, Bristol by Bristol test pilots, most of them ex-RAF instructors. Because he had not been through the normal pilot training, he hadn't officially been given his 'Wings'. At times this caused trouble. Once he even had his pay docked though he had been flying in the RAF for months. It took time, but finally everything was put right. Even 50 years later it still rankles a bit. Even though he flew all through the war, he was not officially classified as a qualified pilot. He arrived in Doncaster early in 1940 to fly Bombays, Ford Trimotors and the 'Italian jobs'.

He recalled the trip to Istres. On the way they called at Bordeaux where he saw some Savoia-Marchetti, ex-Sabena, flown by crews in civilian clothes filling their aircraft by hand from four-gallon drums. He was in a French Air Force mess when the armistice was signed and got hostile looks from the French. This was at Istres, and after a few days, it was decided that they should get back to England. They woke up one morning and the French had disappeared. It was time to go home. There was a number of RAF personnel, too many to be carried home in their aircraft. The crew got into the cockpit, invited as many as could to get in - and to give the pilots a knock when they were ready. Because the Germans occupied the northern half of France, they flew over the Pyrenees and to save fuel they had to fly with a weak mixture - which caused the engines to over-heat. They made it to Bordeaux, which was not occupied, in order to refuel. Cresswell Viney was co-pilot and watched while his captain drew a revolver and forced some French airmen to man the petrol bowser and refuel his aircraft. They were not going to waste time with four-gallon drums. They were still flying on a weak mixture with temperature readings very high - in his terms it was 'shit or bust'. As they reached the English coast, they came across units of the Royal Navy and were challenged to give the colours of the day. They had no idea what they were. Fortunately a Royal Navy Swordfish (he thinks) flew alongside and indicated the right colours. They quickly followed suit.

On arriving back in England, they were met by police. After all that flying they looked a dishevelled lot and badly wanted a bath. The police were the last straw. Cresswell put his bag on the table and told them to do what they wanted with it and left. That night he went to the mess and ordered a pint, but he had only French francs. Standing next to him was the policeman who had met him on landing. He paid for his beer.

When they got back to Doncaster, they were none too popular. They had been posted missing. Doncaster should have been kept informed as to what they were doing. The people at Doncaster were still working on a peace-time base - it keeps the paperwork straight. They had also altered the rear wheel without permission. So much for a peaceful trip to the south of France and returning to welcoming open arms.

This peacetime mentality spread throughout the RAF. At another station they had to line all the aircraft up, forget the enemy, the place must be neat and tidy. In fact, at a bomber station in Yorkshire, the Station Commander had all the bombers lined up when German aircraft appeared. The Germans had a field day.

Though it was a fortnight since the British evacuation of Dunkirk and almost a week after the fall of Paris, aircraft from Doncaster were still flying to France and bringing back personnel and anything else of value. But 271 Squadron's continental operations were coming to an end. One of the last sorties was to Nantes. The aircraft refuelled at Jersey, leaving there on the return trip on June 21 just before the German occupation.

With the fall of France, the squadron had time to regroup and the detachment at Hendon returned home. In addition to its duties in France, the squadron had also been engaged in moving fighter squadrons from the front-line stations in the south to quieter areas. Its equipment was rather a hodgepodge. Besides the Bombays and Harrows which had borne the brunt of the work over France, the squadron had the Ford Trimotor, which was soon to be lost in an accident in County Down, Northern Ireland, and a variety of smaller aircraft, including a Whitney Straight, a small two-seater used by the pilots for any old job (even the odd 'pleasure' flight). At the time no one on the squadron knew much about the history of the aircraft. Even today, for pilots who flew the plane, it remains a mystery. Whitney Straight had been a famous racing driver at Brooklands and he also owned a number of flying clubs in the south. He asked Miles Aircraft to build him a training aircraft for his clubs and this aircraft, one of about 30, was the result.

For 271 Squadron, the next phase of the war was about to begin.

With the fall of France and the Low Countries, Doncaster was a haven for many escaping civilian aircraft. On one day alone, June 19, a mixed bag of 30 aircraft arrived. Others followed, but none stayed long.

There has been a lot of talk over the years about the date of the start of the Battle of Britain but as far as 271 Squadron was concerned there was little or no respite after the Battle of France. The main task for the next few months was in helping Fighter Command rotate their squadrons, a task they had been doing since the outbreak of war. Cresswell Viney reminisces about those exciting and dangerous times in the light-hearted way that was to become the hallmark of the pilots of his generation. He recalls with pleasure the day he spent evacuating fighter squadrons from the front-line fighter airfield at Eastchurch, on the Isle of Sheppey, Kent, to Hornchurch, Essex - backwards and forwards all day. The base at Eastchurch had been badly damaged by bombing. Pilots had to avoid the craters and keep an eye out for German fighters. A few days later he moved a Defiant squadron into the battle area. Then, shortly afterwards, he went back to pick up the remains!

The Defiant was a single-engined fighter with an armament of four machine guns in a power-operated turret behind the pilot's cockpit. It bore some resemblance, head-on, to a Hawker Hurricane and was frequently mistaken as such by the Luftwaffe pilots during these first encounters. They soon got the measure of it and in later battles the Defiants suffered many losses.

On a number of occasions, 271 Squadron had the job of moving Doncaster's other squadron, 616. These and the other removal jobs may sound an easy undertaking but there were difficulties, as these few examples illustrate.

On August 17, a Harrow left Doncaster for Drem, Scotland, to take 602, another auxiliary squadron, to Tangmere. A few minutes after leaving Tangmere, the station was attacked by 30 JU87 dive bombers.

The Harrow would have been a sitting duck if the Germans had been a little earlier or the Harrow a little later.

A more serious incident had happened two days earlier. 234 (Madras) Squadron was to be moved from St. Eval in Cornwall to Middle Wallop, Hampshire. Two Bombays carried an advance party of ground staff and after a flight of one and a half hours they arrived at Middle Wallop in the middle of a dog fight between Spitfires of 234 Squadron and German fighters. In spite of the battle, the Bombays made two attempts to land but were warned off by a very brave man who dashed out of the control tower firing 'verey' lights. The Bombays took the hint and moved off, landing safely at nearby Boscombe Down. The controllers at Boscombe Down had been watching their attempts to land and had expected the aircraft to have been shot down or at the very least forced down. Half an hour later the Bombays took off and finally landed at Middle Wallop. The pilots were Polish and there is no record of the comments made by their passengers, but whatever they might have said, it was unlikely they would have been under-stood. On another occasion, a Bom-bay was not so lucky - it was destroyed on the ground at St. Eval, though without casual-ties.

During the Battle of Britain there was hardly a fighter station that wasn't

H.P. 42 Helena in rather more RAFM
gracious times and before her hard landing
at Donibristle after which her remains were used as an office

visited by the squadron, from Wick in the north to St. Eval in the south-west, so much so they were often called 'RAF's Pickfords'. Most of this work was done by the Bombays and the Harrows but sometimes the HP42s joined in.

On August 1, an HP42 (Helena by name) left Doncaster and after a hard landing at Donibristle, Scotland, was so badly damaged that it had to be dismantled. The Royal Navy did the job. They mounted the metal-clad part of the fuselage on a wooden cradle and used it as an office.

There was more bad news to come. On an run-of-the-mill operation taking ammunition from Ringway to Stornaway, another HP42 - the one called Horsa - got into trouble when its two port engines cut out and it had to force-land. As it landed, one of its starboard engines caught fire and the crew had just enough time to escape before the fuel tanks exploded.

So ended Helena and Horsa, two of the queens of the air. After all the glamorous flying between the capitals of Europe, they had ended their days as RAF workhorses.

With the Battle of Britain raging all over the south coast, fears of invasion were rife. Once again all leave was cancelled at Doncaster and those on leave recalled. Further troops arrived to help defend the airfield. Cresswell Viney remembers that they were flying during the day and spent the night helping to man the pill boxes - but at least they could talk to one another with the internal telephone system, the kind you had to wind up.

Cresswell Viney was selected to take his Harrow to Farnborough to have a three-ton magnet fitted underneath his aircraft - the idea being to fly over the North Sea and blow up magnetic mines. Unfortunately, the magnet upset the compass - which meant that you had to fly over the sea without a compass and still try to find the mines. It was all good fun, but the idea was dropped. Cresswell Viney left Doncaster soon after the experiment with the magnet and spent the rest of the war touring the world. He ended his service at Finningley as armament officer and then rejoined the reserves. He was awarded the Air Efficiency Award and Bar. It is only given to long-service volunteer reservists. He says that he got two because war service counts twice. "It's not really called the bar, but something else, but whatever it is called, I've got it. It's a nice medal with your name on it. But all you had to do was to stay alive and keep your nose clean, or at least not be found out." Cresswell served 16 years from 1937 to 1953.

It had been decided that the airfield was too small for operational fighters and bombers. The runways were short and there were too many houses nearby. But it remained the home of a transport squadron, and as such was host to many VIPs, who usually needed a guard of honour. It created its own brand of crisis, 'when the C-in-C Home forces arrives, forget the invasion, the station has to get its priorities right and its best coat on.' The guards of honour were usually provided by station headquarters. They must have been the smartest headquarters staff

DH 91 Albatross 'Franklin' based at Doncaster until it was damaged beyond repair in an accident in Iceland. Her sister aircraft 'Faraday' was also based at Doncaster and suffered a similar fate.

in the RAF, to match the well-painted and 'spit and polish' surroundings. Besides the C-in-C Home Forces, in quick succession came the Admiral Commanding Home Fleet, a sprinkling of Government Ministers plus many other senior officers. They all had to be entertained. On occasion, usually because of bad weather or mechanical break-down, they had to stay the night. When the Chief of the Imperial General Staff is staying the night, or just calling for a cup of tea, it tends to curb the spirits of the bravest souls. Many years later, Group Captain Glover was of the opinion that the number of visits by the top brass was not because his squadron was a transport squadron but because everyone was so impressed with its efficiency.

By the end of September, the threat of invasion was judged to have receded. Many of the defending troops left and the Royal Engineers bricked up some of the pill boxes - there were not enough people to man them. Other duties emerged. Anti-submarine bases had been set up in Iceland and the squadron was called upon to provide transport, carrying stores and mail between Wick, Scotland, and Reykjavik. The squadron started operating these services to Reykjavik in October 1940, flying a type of aircraft new to the squadron, the DH91 Albatross. Early in 1941 it was joined by another Albatross. Both were still known by their civilian names, 'Faraday' and 'Franklin'. They had the classical lines of a De Havilland aircraft, the same lines that were to be seen many years later in the world's first jet airliner, the Comet. For the short period they were at Doncaster, they could be seen by passers-by parked in the corner of the airfield by Stott's garage. These two aircraft put Doncaster and the squadron back on the international air map, but their time was short. Both aircraft came to grief in accidents at Reykjavik. They were replaced by an American Lockheed Hudson, yet another new type for the squadron.

The station maintained its local connections. It supplied teams to the

Handley Page Harrow blown over 6th December 1940   RAFM
with Prince's Road in background

local sports leagues and it was not unknown for local ladies to be entertained in the various messes, all strictly above board of course. One of the local newspapers, The Sheffield Telegraph and Star, collected funds to provide those little extras that servicemen, away from home, appreciate especially at Christmas time. Punch's Hotel in the south and the Park Hotel in the north became the airfield's 'locals', further integrating the airforce and the town. Airforce police patrolled the town centre, but there was very little trouble and the relationship between the squadron and the town was such that the squadron thought of themselves as 'Doncaster's Own'. This friendly relationship was not always apparent and at times did not extend to the guard room on Ellers Road. One dark

night Bernard Cuttriss, a local businessman and historian, who was chief warden for Bessacarr, saw what he thought was a light showing from the domestic quarters of the airfield and told the guards to 'Put that light out'. The guards were not amused and detained him for several hours until his identity was proved.

The second Christmas of the war was approaching but the weather was not in the festive spirit. On the evening of December 6, 1940, a fierce gale lashed the airfield and created almost as much damage to the squadron as the enemy had

H.P. 42 Hadrian after gale   RAFM
of 6th December 1940 on the mineral line
where it runs parallel to Stoops Lane

done. A Harrow was blown over on what is now the Ellers School playing fields. This aircraft had a mysterious past (more of that later) but even sadder was the fate of HP42, Hadrian. It was blown over onto the mineral line on the

Westland Lysander 17 of which had been built   G. H. Oakes
at Doncaster. They had equipped 613 (City of Manchester) Squadron before changing over to the Mustang

eastern side of the airfield. Despite the combined efforts of a large number of men, one of whom broke a leg, the wind got under the aircraft a second time and it was finally deposited in a field on the opposite side of the railway line. This was the end of the line for the HP42s. Three had come to Doncaster, one had crashed at Whitehaven, one dismantled after a heavy landing and now the survivor had been blown to pieces. Eight of these majestic aircraft had been built and Hadrian had been the last.

On the same night another Harrow was destroyed in the same gale at Scampton - it was a very poor night for the squadron. Because of the havoc caused by the gale, the Air Ministry decided to install 18 hard standings, commonly called panhandles. These would enable aircraft to be more securely fastened down.

The mysterious Harrow blown over in the gale had been painted black and had only recently returned to Doncaster after spending some time away. During the Battle of Britain any idea that might help bring down German bombers was taken seriously. Someone somewhere had thought up the wheeze that if an aircraft trailed half-mile lengths of piano wire with a small bomb fastened on the end, it could fly over any convenient German bomber and gently guide the bomb on to it. The Harrow was the aircraft chosen to do the experimental work, which was given the code name 'Mutton' (in the hope, presumably, that the enemy aircraft it attacked would be as dead as mutton). The idea was abandoned after an incident

Vickers Wellington many built and repaired   G. H. Oakes
at the Ministry of Aircraft Production Factory at Doncaster

in which all the bombs inside the Harrow exploded by accident and without causing significant damage. The RAF worked out that if all the bombs exploding together inside the aircraft did little damage what chance was there of a single bomb exploding outside destroying a German bomber? The aircraft returned to Doncaster, only to be blown over.

The magnet and mutton ideas were not the only experimental schemes in which the Harrow had been involved. In 1938, Sir Alan Cobham, well-known to Doncaster, had used a Harrow in the world's first in-flight refuelling when he transferred 920 gallons of fuel from a Harrow to an Imperial Airways 'C' class flying boat, Cambria, over Southampton. It was the forerunner of much greater things.

The night of December 6 was not the only time that high winds caused trouble. John Glover tells of another night of high winds when he was on his rounds checking that everything was in order. He came across one of the HP42s airborne several feet off the ground, though still tied down. The engines were rotating backwards because of the lack of compression.

He climbed on board and saw that the airspeed indicator was showing flying speed because of the wind flowing across the instruments. He then had to go through the normal procedures of landing the aircraft. There are not many pilots who have landed more times than they have taken off.

After the fall of France and the ending of the Battle of Britain, the squadron settled down to a mundane sort of life and spent its time fetching and carrying for anyone who needed such a service. Amongst other duties, it operated a service to the very north of Scotland and the Outer Islands, taking supplies and personnel. This became known as the 'Cabbage Run'.

One such flight is recorded by Newton Foster, an airborne fitter with 271 Squadron and now, 50 years later, still living in Doncaster. He recalls leaving Prestwick in a Harrow in December, 1940 for the Isle of Man en route for Doncaster. After landing on the island, the pilot requested fuel. The airman in charge of the refuelling assured the pilot that he knew how to refuel the Harrow. The flight home started in good weather but as they neared home the weather closed in and the pilot had great difficulty in finding his position, despite flying closer to the ground. Suddenly the engines started losing power and the aircraft finally crashed at Grimethorpe, breaking its back. All the crew were hurt. The seriously injured were taken to hospital in Wakefield and the less seriously hurt to a military hospital at Nostell Priory. The most seriously hurt was a military policeman who had 'thumbed' a lift in the Isle of Man. He lived in Liverpool, but it was easier to travel home from Doncaster than to wait for a boat. It turned out that the accident happened because petrol had been put into the engine oil tanks. The man responsible for the refuelling was subsequently court-martialled.

Meanwhile the factory on the airfield had stopped producing Lysanders - the contract to build 500 had been cancelled and only 17 were built. A company called Phillips & Powis in collaboration with Miles Aircraft planned to use the site to build the Miles Master, a small training aircraft. However, because of production difficulties, only one aircraft was made.

The factory was then taken over by Brooklands Aviation of Weybridge.

Bill Woodford, still living in Doncaster, had been a joiner with Ward Brothers of Waterdale and was drafted into the aircraft factory along with many others. If you were a joiner in Doncaster, that was almost certainly your fate. He joined the factory when it was operated by Westlands. Later he was employed by Brooklands Aviation. This company had operated a factory at Lindholme for the previous six months and had started to manufacture Wellington bombers. Before they could complete one, they were moved, staff and all, to Doncaster.

Wellingtons, designed by Barnes Wallis of Dambusters fame, were made partly of wood, so there was a great demand for joiners. In the aircraft's 'geodetic' design, wooden slats were built around the fuselage so the fabric covering could be attached. Several other parts were also made of wood. The completed bombers were air-tested at Doncaster - one of them crashed on to Bawtry Road near the racecourse. For some days it was a centre of attraction for the locals, particularly the hordes of small boys who wanted a piece as a souvenir. The police soon put a stop to that.

Bill Woodford tells of damaged bombers coming to Doncaster to be repaired after being shot up on bombing raids. Some of them contained sad remains which had to be cleared out before work could be started.

Every morning and afternoon, St. Cecilia's Road was full of cyclists on their way to or from the factory. In those days few, if any, workers had cars and if they had there was a little matter of petrol or rather the lack of it. The usual entrance to the factory was through a ginnel, a passage, from St. Cecilia's Road, guarded by a single policeman.

Another of the workers at the factory was Stanley Sands then, as now, living in Dunsville. He had started at Lindholme working with Brooklands Aviation and had moved with them when they moved to Doncaster taking a half-completed Wellington with them. He puts staff numbers at between 300 and 350. He thinks that they built about 150 bombers (Bill Woodford remembers lower numbers all round). Whichever is more correct, if the number of repaired bombers is taken into account, Doncaster made a hefty contribution to the bomber offensive against Germany.

Stanley Sands was in a team that went to crash sites to recover parts of aircraft that could be used again. He also expresses his sadness at the very large number of aircraft that crashed in the Doncaster area. He tells of one occasion when three Halifaxes crashed around Dunsville and of a Halifax crashing on or near the decoy airfield at Holme Wood Lane. He thought there were about 16 on board, including ferry pilots. Councillor John Meredith also saw a Halifax crash, south of Dunsville. There were few,

From the Führer's Speech

Leaflet dropped by the Germans on Bessacarr autumn 1940

if any, survivors - some were killed when they tried to jump out just before the aircraft came down.

At all times, the armed forces are willing to help any civilian in distress and needing help. Later this was to be known as 'Aid to the Civil Community'. So, when a Lady (capital 'L') brought her problems to John Glover, who was now both Squadron and Station Commander, he was too much of a gentleman to refuse. Lady Warncliffe's desperate problem was that the Ecclesfield Beagle Hunt, of which she was the master, had nowhere to keep their beagles. There happened to be an empty building that could be made suitable and suddenly the hounds had a new home. The groom also found a roof over his head. The beagles were exercised on the racecourse - it would not have been the done thing to allow them to wander over the runways, their Lordships at the Air Ministry would not have approved. It was also rumoured that they were carried around by a lorry provided by the RAF. After a while the accommodation was required for WAAFs and the hounds left for a local farm. It was, of course, just a coincidence that the Station Commander was a hunt enthusiast.

John Glover tells of the trips he and other pilots made to Ringway, Manchester, to drop parachutists. But there was a problem. When the parachutists left the aircraft, they often tore the fabric covering on the Harrow. So, as soon as possible, the operations were cancelled.

Newton Foster, an airborne fitter, also remembers the drops. He thought the whole thing odd. The men they were dropping were all civilians. Why were civilians being trained in parachuting? Perhaps they were to be dropped secretly in occupied Europe. But the trips were enjoyable.

The aircraft left Doncaster very early in the morning, picked up the trainee parachutists, dropped them, and was back home in time for breakfast.

Aerial activity over Doncaster was not confined to the RAF - ever since the early days of the war, German aircraft had flown over the area. In the autumn of 1940, leaflets were found in Bessacarr reporting a speech by Adolf Hitler. The next objects to be dropped by the Germans were rather more lethal. On the night of December 12/13, 1940, the Germans heavily bombed Sheffield. Perhaps because one of the aircraft had lost its bearing, a line of small bombs was dropped near Wilby Farm, now Rose Hill Crematorium. A week later, more bombs fell at Hexthorpe on the LNER's Eden Grove Sports Ground and the nearby works. Over the next few months, bombs were scattered over Doncaster, including the airfield and adjacent roads. Sandbeck Road, Thoresby Avenue, Clumber Road, Chequer Avenue, Lime Tree Avenue, Stockhill Road and Theobald Avenue all suffered. So did Balby Carr Bank and parts of Bentley, including the area behind the Sun Inn Hotel. Most of these bombs were small; others were canisters of incendiaries. Some of the bombs failed to explode, and little damage was done.

However, Doncaster's relative immunity to bombing ended on the night of May 8/9, 1941 when aerial mines - large canisters suspended on a parachute - were dropped on four sites in Doncaster. Two fell in the Weston Road area, one in Weston Road and the other near Loversall Hospital. These two bombs caused 16 deaths. 73 people were injured, 31 seriously. 13 houses were destroyed and another 19 had to be demolished and a further 414 were damaged. The other two mines were dropped in Bessacarr, one close to St. Wilfrid's Road near Whin Hill Road and the other on Ellers Avenue. These two bombs killed two people and injured five. Five houses were either destroyed or had to be demolished later. 152 others were damaged and many others had windows broken. This was the worst night of German bombing, but not the last. On September 1, 1942, two 500kg bombs fell on the town centre, one on Station Road in front of the Grand Theatre and the other in West Street, killing two people and injuring five. Windows were broken over a wide area and the large panes of glass in the Co-op were broken, exposing meat in the butchery department. On the same night, smaller bombs were dropped on the

railway, setting a building on fire and causing the main line to be diverted for a while.

Doncaster had little more bombing

North American Mustang which equipped both 613 (City of Manchester) and 169 Squadrons   G. H. Oakes

during the rest of the war. Some small bombs were dropped over Belle Vue but they caused no damage. Some were also dropped on the airport but were too insignificant even to be reported in the official RAF diary.

During the entire war, 20 people were killed by bombing in Doncaster and another 83 injured. 38 houses were destroyed and nearly 900 damaged. These figures represent tragedy for so many families, but compared with other towns and cities, Doncaster escaped lightly.

Every year throughout the second world war, there was a campaign to raise funds to build weapons for the war effort. People were encouraged to save money in National Savings and the money was used to buy ships, aircraft etc. One year, Doncaster raised enough money to buy a destroyer, HMS Lightning. Unfortunately, she was torpedoed in the Mediterranean by a German U-Boat - there is a commemorative plaque in the Mansion House. The town and surrounding villages adopted a replacement, HMS Zephyr, which survived the war.

Other weeks were dedicated to 'Wings for Victory' with Spitfires as the usual target. But there was another way in which people could make a direct contribution to the war effort and that was to buy a ship or aircraft outright. A group of Doncaster people paid for a Spitfire which served in 403 (RCAF) and 54 squadrons. It ended its fighting career on September 17, 1941 when it crashed into the English Channel while on patrol.

In July, 1941, 613 (City of Manchester) Squadron arrived after a short flight from Firbeck, a small grass airfield, ten miles to the south west. 613 Squadron had been formed as an auxiliary squadron at Ringway, Manchester, on March 1, 1939, and equipped with Hawker Hind biplanes as an army co-operation unit. In April 1940, the squadron was based at Odiham in Hampshire and equipped with Westland Lysanders. After the German invasion of France and the Low Countries, every available aircraft was pressed into service and the squadron had its first taste of action when six Lysanders operating out of Hawkinge in Kent attacked German heavy field guns near Calais. The Lysander, of which 17 had been built at Doncaster in the early part of the war, was a very slow single-engined aircraft with an outstanding ability for short landings and take-offs in rough fields. It was used, for instance, to fly agents into France. It had been designed as an army cooperation spotter aircraft. If attacked by an enemy fighter, no matter how old-fashioned, its chances of survival were slim.

With the collapse of France, the squadron in June 1940 moved to Netherthorpe near Worksop and in November it moved again to Firbeck. In August 1941, while at Doncaster, it was again re-equipped, this time with American Curtis Tomahawks, a single-engined fighter. It moved again, to Andover, but only for a fortnight before it returned to Doncaster. In April 1942. it was re-equipped with North American Mustangs and moved to Twinwood Farm. It achieved its greatest successes in the latter part of the war when it was based at Lasham in Hampshire and re-equipped with De Havilland Mosquitoes. Possibly its most famous operation was in April 1944 when its Mosquitoes attacked and destroyed the Gestapo Headquarters at The Hague. The attack was made by six Mosquitoes. Later reconnaissance photographs showed that the target had been reduced to rubble with neighbouring houses untouched. Similar raids were made on Gestapo Headquarters in other European cities but few, if any, were so accurate. Both Netherthorpe and Firbeck were under the overall control of Doncaster and after 613 Squadron had left, both stations were placed on a 'Care and Maintenance' basis and their landing areas temporarily blocked.

Bomb-disposal units had come to Doncaster in the earlier part of the war. In addition to a bomb-disposal squadron, a senior organisation - a Wing - had arrived in October 1941 with the men accommodated in Eastfield House, part of the Deaf School, and the officers in Hillcrest, Bawtry Road, now a residential home with a new name. The new arrivals triggered a general moving around. The old Tote Building in Wheatley Hills became part of the sick bay, the sick quarters at Whitegates became officers quarters and the sick bay at Saxton Avenue became quarters for WAAF officers.

Doncaster's bomb-disposal units were responsible for handling emergencies in the greater part of the North of England. They dealt with bombs dropped by the Germans, but they also had the task of neutralising any bombs found in crashed or damaged allied bombers. They were also called on to help with other kinds of bomb problem. There was a disastrous incident at Snaith, a bomber base, just to the north of Doncaster. In 1943, the bomb dump there exploded, killing 17 people, most of them Canadians. The dump contained many primed delayed-action bombs so the whole area had to be evacuated for seven days, the maximum 'delay' time. Meanwhile, other bombs kept on exploding at regular intervals, throwing shrapnel over a distance of a mile and a half from the base. To protect the nearby village, the Doncaster units built a blast wall around the dump, a very courageous act. After a week, they went into what was left of the dump to make safe the remaining unfused bombs.

This dump was not the only one in the area to explode. The dump at Melbourne, a bomber base a few miles north of Snaith, also exploded - with the loss of 18 lives, though this time there were no delayed-action bombs to deal with. The bomb-disposal units stayed at Doncaster until after the war ended when they moved to Abbots Ripton.

The importance of the facilities at Doncaster and at nearby Lindholme and Finningley to the RAF was appreciated by the Air Ministry and to help protect them they constructed a decoy airfield at the bottom of Holme Wood Lane, Armthorpe, now the site of a sewerage works. It was designed to confuse approaching German bombers. Lights were arranged to give the impression of runways, and during the day the buildings and dummy aircraft gave every appearance of a functioning airfield.

On August 29, 1941, a Harrow got into trouble near home over Darrington. It had engine trouble and made a forced landing into a barley field. Repair vehicles arrived from Doncaster and after a short stay the Harrow was on its way back to Doncaster leaving only two pairs of tracks through the barley.

By September 1941, a number of aircraft had been lost through enemy action and several more others by accident. Gales had already cost the squadron dearly and another struck the station in October 1941. The value of the close connections with the local authority was shown yet again when the RAF turned to the Borough Surveyor, Mr Ford, for help in rehousing personnel whose tents had been blown down. Mr. Ford had been responsible for the airfield from the very beginning in the early thirties. The Air Ministry put their thanks on record for this further help.

169 Squadron was formed on June 15, 1942 at Twinwood Farm as a tactical reconnaissance unit of Army Co-operation Command. It received its first aircraft, North American Mustangs, from 613 Squadron. Twelve days after being formed, it moved to Doncaster to start its operational training. It went to Weston Zoyland for a few days in October, returned to Doncaster until November 15 when it moved to Clifton. After being re-equipped with Mosquitoes, it spent the rest of the war as an intruder force, clearing the way for British night bombers in the offensive over Europe. It was disbanded at Great Massington on August 10, 1945.

In the autumn of 1942, 271 Squadron was given another task. A number of Harrows were detached to Netherhaven to give airborne troops further experience of air travel and map-reading. Experiments into air sickness were also carried out.

Pilots in 271 Squadron led a peripatetic life. For example, J.V. Venn who spent three years as a pilot with the Squadron at Doncaster, says that during his time there he visited 153 airfields, transporting service personnel, stores and anything else that needed moving. One of his first flights was to Prestwick, then a grass airfield with a hotel in the corner. The airfield had been taken over and the staff drafted into the services, the chief booking clerk becoming a Flight Lieutenant. Life for Mr. Venn was pleasant but a little boring, though one of his trips was rather more interesting - as he explains.

The squadron was ordered to send two Harrows to Dyce to ferry stores to Thornaby. The Squadron Commander thought this a pleasant day's outing. Thornaby was just up the road from Doncaster, and he decided to take one of the Harrows, Venn took the other. However when they arrived at Dyce, they were told that the stores had to go to Stornoway, not Thornaby. There was no airfield at Stornoway, just a golf course. When they reached Stornoway, they saw a ship on fire in the harbour. This was a shock but not a problem for them. Their problem was there were no starting motors and they had great difficulty in getting the engines going in the morning. Still they managed and returned safely to Doncaster leaving some heavily pock-marked fairways. The Squadron Commander was not at all pleased. He had looked for a pleasant day's flying. He got more than that and he hadn't even taken his golf clubs.

Ron Williams, also a pilot with 271 Squadron, arrived in Doncaster in 1943. Like most other pilots he remembers flying the Whitney Straight, but knew little about it. It was useful for odd jobs and for 'keeping your hand in'. There was also a mixed bag of other aircraft - the Harrows, a few Oxfords, a Dominie (the RAF version of the DH 89 Rapide), a Tiger Moth and a Proctor.

The greater part of Ron Williams' work was the 'Cabbage Run'. "We were not fussy what and whom we carried. If they asked we took them - if we had room." One of Ron's passengers was Jim Mollinson, one-time husband of the world-famous air pioneer, Amy Johnson. Jim came from Hull. He had made a number of record breaking flights himself and "there he was, sitting behind me".

Flying the Cabbage Run up in the north of Scotland was a fairly primitive business. Aids were few, if any. Pilots had to find their own way, often leaning out of the window to see where they were. Fortunately, the Harrow was very reliable and easy to fly, even on one engine. It had excellent gliding characteristics but it was very draughty and noisy. In the north of Scotland, they had to fly in all weathers, but flying above the clouds and the weather was dangerous - "you didn't know what was underneath and we didn't even have windscreen wipers or parachutes. The passengers didn't have parachutes either. Islands were useful land marks, so was the Old Man of Hoy. If you missed that you were on your way to Iceland, or worse. Besides the Cabbage Run, we were still being used to rotate fighter squadrons."

To show how dangerous it was flying in and around the Outer Islands, Ron Williams recalls two Harrows crashing, one at Auchinblae, Kincardineshire, now Grampians, and the other at Inishowen Head, Co Donegal. He didn't know why the aircraft crashed in the Republic of Ireland. It was not supposed to be there, but navigation aids were very primitive and it must have been off course, using Inishowen Head as a land mark and flew too close.

There weren't many aids to flying at Doncaster either. Landing there during daylight was straightforward. At night, without any form of lighting, an extra bit of skill was needed. Says Ron, "You had the roads and railway lines that reflected the moonlight and if there was no air raid in progress there where some red lights on the hangars".

In March 1943, Transport Command had been formed and 271 Squadron became part of the new formation. With the invasion of Europe in mind, a number of new transport squadrons were formed to carry the ever-growing number of airborne troops. In August 1943 the first of the Dakotas were flown in from Prestwick, Scotland by the squadron's own pilots. There was a steady build-up in numbers and by the beginning of 1944, the squadron had 30 Dakotas. The conversion to the new aircraft was the responsibility of the new squadron commander, Wing Commander Booth DFC and bar, who had assumed command in September 1943.

In the early hours of September 9, 1943, Doncaster was informed that a Halifax bomber had crashed near Mount Pleasant and the station fire services were sent to the scene together with medical personnel. They stayed for over an hour until relieved by units from Finningley.

The Sommerfeld tracking exposed in
1990 when building the Dome car park   G. Blaik

In January 1944, nearly 1,000 yards of Sommerfeld tracking was laid on Doncaster's NE/SW runway. Sommer-feld track-ing was a steel mesh that was unrolled and laid on the grass. The grass could grow through, but the surface remained stabilised and could take heavier aircraft in most weathers. It was used extensively in France, after the invasion, to build temporary airfields. A specially equipped lorry, or lorries, drove along where the runway was needed unrolling the tracking - and hey-presto, a runway.

The tracking at Doncaster was forgotten about by the powers that be. When they came to build the car park for the Dome nearly 50 years later, they found it!

On January 10, 1944, 'B' Flight of 271 Squadron was formed into 569 Squadron, the third squadron to emerge at Doncaster during the war. It never became operational and was suspended on March 1, 1944. Its personnel returned to 271 Squadron, again as 'B' Flight.

Dakotas were now coming across the Atlantic in large numbers. Many had to be modified to meet the requirements of 43 Group Army Support and a conversion unit was formed at Doncaster to do the work. At times the station was converting eight a day. Losses were fewer than expected and finally 30 spare aircraft were sent to Pershore for storage.

Aerial view of RAF Doncaster 16th July 1944. Experts say there are about Barry Thomson
100 aircraft present, mainly Dakotas. Note prison of war camp, bottom right hand corner,
in the silver ring of the racecourse. The prisoners had free entry but no temporary exit passes. The
grandstands were used by the Royal Veterinary Corps, who are commemorated by a plaque in the new
grandstand, and the present Town Moor Golf course was used for food production. The RAF HF/DF
station is on the inside of the running track by the bend near Rose Hill.

On February 11, 1944. two officers from Doncaster were sent to inspect a new airfield at Down Ampney in Wiltshire. It had only a few buildings but three hard runways. With these, the airfield was more suitable for operating heavier aircraft than Doncaster was, and it was closer to France. The squadron moved to its new base there on February 28, though 'D' Flight, still equipped with Sparrows, stayed behind. Although most of the squadron no longer played a part in the history of Doncaster, mention must be made of what happened to it over the next year or so. It must be remembered that the squadron thought of itself as 'Doncaster's Own' and the training that prepared them for their duties in France had been undertaken at Doncaster.

Each RAF squadron had to keep an Operation Record Book, an official record of the squadron's activities. Keeping these records was obviously a chore, something that had to be done as quickly as possible. No effort was made to differentiate between major and minor happenings, such as the crash of an aircraft with total loss of life and the posting in of a new squadron member. Each page was lined with columns, all with headings, and had to be filled in as per Air Ministry instructions. Any deviation to the laid-down procedure must signify an unusual event and the entry in the squadron's Operation Record Book for June 5, 1944 showed that the squadron's Intelligence Officer appreciated the importance of the day. He filled in, not the normal factual entry, but something more suitable for the occasion. This is what he reported just a few hours after the event.

DAY OF DAYS

The briefing of crews for operation TONGA, which is part of the main operation OVERLORD, was divided into two parts. At 15.00 seven tug and glider crews assembled in the briefing room. The crews had been given a general outline of the operations as a whole on June 3 and this was the final briefing. The mission of these crews was to release at CT (Civil Twilight) 4.35 on D DAY seven gliders on DZ (Drop Zone) called

Flight Lieutenant David Lord V.C. flying over Burma in a DC 2K   Frank Lord

'V'. At the time of the briefing the weather did not appear too promising but the Meteorologist Officer gave an encouraging report and said there would be a general improvement and the weather would be quite good at the time of the operation. Fortunately this proved to be quite correct. Briefing was carried out very carefully and finally the Commanding Officer read out a message from Air Chief Marshal Leigh Mallory wishing everybody the best of luck. At 17.00, briefing commenced for the paradropping part of the operation. TONGA 39 crews (nine from 271 squadron and 30 from 48 squadron) were detailed to drop the main body of the 3rd Parachute Brigade at CT 4.30 on the same DZ. At 21.50 a great convoy of lorries full of paratroops was seen streaming round the perimeter track en route for the various aircraft neatly marshalled on the aerodrome. All the paradropping planes were filled with 12 20lb GP (General Purpose) ready to give a little surprise for the enemy troops operating the coastal defences. Approximately 20 paratroops had been allocated to each paradropping plane. The morale of the boys was just perfect - a more cheerful and determined body of men could not have been selected for the job.

Very few men were being carried in the gliders as these had been packed with a variety of equipment including jeeps, trailers, guns, motor-cycles etc. Just previous to the take-off, the Commanding Officer dashed round to every plane to deliver personally a message from General Eisenhower. The first glider tugging aircraft flown by W.C. Booth DFC took off at 22.48 and No 1 paradropping plane started at 23.20. The results of the squadron's first operational trip would unquestionably play a most important part in the successful part in the kick-off of the invasion of Europe. At 02.30, June 6, the first aircraft touched down at base followed by a stream of other planes. The glider-tug crews reported all gliders were released in the vicinity of the LZ (Landing Zone) at heights ranging from 1,000 to 1,700 ft. The majority of the paratroops were dropped in the DZ and none were estimated to have dropped more than 300 yards away. Of the 725 paratroops carried, 722 were dropped. The remaining three were brought back due to sickness or injury. 271 Squadron carried out and dropped 165 paratroops in carrying aircraft and 20 paratroops in the gliders. The operation was a complete success and completed without the loss of a single aircraft (one injured paratrooper had been accidentally shot in the aircraft).

Christmas card drawn by Jimmy Edwards for 271 Squadron 1943

Newton Foster

When the Dakotas had first come to Doncaster, many new crew members had also arrived and started training for the squadron's new role of troop-carrying and para-dropping. One of these newcomers was Flight Lieutenant K. O. Edwards, later better known as the comedian 'Professor Jimmy Edwards'. Because of the shortage of accommodation for officers, he was billeted with Mrs Moon at 18 Ellers Road, opposite the airmen's temporary camp and five houses away from No 28 which

Jimmy Edwards being interviewed by Dutch TV at British Airborne cemetery in Oosterbeek

Alan Hartley

had been destroyed by an enemy bomb in May 1941. Jimmy Edwards left Doncaster with the squadron to join in 'Overlord', the invasion of Europe. On September 20, 1944 he took part in operation 'Market', the airborne phase of 'Market Garden', when the 1st British Airborne Division and a Polish Brigade were dropped at Arnhem to capture a vital bridge over the River Rhine. After dropping his supplies, he was attacked by a German fighter and forced to crash-land. The fighter then machine-gunned the survivors on the ground. Jimmy evaded capture and returned to his squadron in December 1944.

For this and other efforts he was awarded the DFC.

Another of the new pilots was Flight Lieutenant David Lord. Although he was already an experienced Dakota pilot, he had to train with a new crew in the techniques of paradropping and glider-towing. Like Jimmy Edwards, he took part in the events on D Day and then helped supply the forces in the Allied bridgehead. On September 19, he flew supplies and ammunition to the beleaguered paratroops at Arnhem. He was soon hit by intense flak and his starboard engine caught fire. In spite of this, he made a run over the dropping zone and dropped part of his load. He could then have flown back to base, but although his engine was on fire and one of the aircraft wings showed signs of breaking off, he went round again with the German gunners concentrating on him. He flew low over the Drop Zone and dropped the remainder of his load. He then ordered his crew to bale out. Seconds later the wing collapsed. There was only one survivor - who was taken prisoner. On November 13, 1945, the King awarded a posthumous Victoria Cross to Flight Lieutenant David Samuel Anthony Lord, RAF, of 271 Squadron.

'D' Flight, with its Sparrow aircraft, had remained at Doncaster when the rest of the squadron had moved to Down Ampney.

In July it moved to Watchfield, Berkshire. Its task for the next few months was to evacuate casualties from the front line to the rear. The Sparrow, first designed and built as a bomber, with its antiquated looks, was now being used for humanitarian purposes. It also out-performed its American successor, the Dakota, in its ability to land and take off from small, unprepared fields.

Whether its operating base was in France or at Watchfield, any aircraft from 271 Squadron that required major servicing, returned to Doncaster. Doncaster had lost its customs and immigration control in 1939 and although the Continent had been occupied for five years there were still many interesting and useful things that could be obtained there and brought home. Doncaster aircraft, manned in many cases by Doncastrians and landing at Doncaster, were involved in a steady and possibly illegal trade.

On January 1, 1945 'D' Flight was based at Evere, Brussels, and in the

FOURTH SUPPLEMENT
TO

The London Gazette

Of FRIDAY, the 9th of NOVEMBER, 1945

published by Authority

Registered as a newspaper

TUESDAY, 13 NOVEMBER, 1945

Air Ministry, 13th November, 1945.

The KING has been graciously pleased to confer the VICTORIA CROSS on the undermentioned officer in recognition of most conspicuous bravery: —

Flight Lieutenant David Samuel Anthony LORD, D.F.C. (49149), R.A.F., 271 Sqn. (deceased).

Flight Lieutenant Lord was pilot and captain of a Dakota aircraft detailed to drop supplies at Arnhem on the afternoon of the 19th September, 1944. Our airborne troops had been surrounded and were being pressed into a small area defended by a large number of anti-aircraft guns. Air crews were warned that intense opposition would be met over the dropping zone. To ensure accuracy they were ordered to fly at 900 feet when dropping their containers.

While flying at 1,500 feet near Arnhem the starboard wing of Flight Lieutenant Lord's aircraft was twice hit by anti-aircraft fire. The starboard engine was set on fire. He would have been justified in leaving the main stream of supply aircraft and continuing at the same height or even abandoning his aircraft. But on learning that his crew were uninjured and that the dropping zone would be reached in three minutes he said he would complete his mission, as the troops were in dire need of supplies.

By now the starboard engine was burning furiously. Flight Lieutenant Lord came down to 900 feet, where he was singled out for the concentrated fire of all the anti-aircraft guns. On reaching the dropping zone he kept the aircraft on a straight and level course while supplies were dropped. At the end of the run, he was told that two containers remained.

Although he must have known that the collapse of the starboard wing could not be long delayed, Flight Lieutenant Lord circled, rejoined the stream of aircraft and made a second run to drop the remaining supplies.

These manoeuvres took eight minutes in all, the aircraft being continuously under heavy anti-aircraft fire.

His task completed, Flight Lieutenant Lord ordered his crew to abandon the Dakota, making no attempt himself to leave the aircraft, which was down to 500 feet. A few seconds later, the starboard wing collapsed and the aircraft fell in flames. There was only one survivor, who was flung out while assisting other members of the crew to put on their parachutes.

By continuing his mission in a damaged and burning aircraft, descending to drop the supplies accurately, returning to the dropping zone a second time and, finally, remaining at the controls to give his crew a chance of escape, Flight Lieutenant Lord displayed supreme valour and self-sacrifice.

Air Ministry, 13th November, 1945.

The KING has been graciously pleased to approve the following awards: —

Distinguished Service Order.

Acting Squadron Leade..
Leonard Charles Cookson HAWKINS, D.F.C (102129), R.A.F.V.R., 135 Sqn.

Distinguished Flying Cross.

Acting Squadron Leade..
Jack Raymond SHEPHERD (100575), R.A.F.V.R., 110 Sqn.

Flight Lieutenants.
Philip BROWN (128568), R.A.F.V.R., 110 Sqn.
John Desmond DUNBAR (130943), R.A.F.V.R
Antony James JACOMB-HOOD (135501), R.A.F.V.R., 47 Sqn.
George Hayward JONES (152650), R.A.F.V.R., 684 Sqn.
David Dougherty WARWICK (48888), R.A.F., 684 Sqn.

Flying Officers.
Douglas Page THOMPSON (135120), R.A.F.V.R., 47 Sqn.
William Raymond WILLIAMS (181010), R.A.F.V.R., 28 Sqn.

early morning the whole of the flight was lined up in readiness for the day's work. Some had their engines running, when out of the dawn came between 100 and 110 German 109s from 26 Jagdgeschwader 11 and 111 Gruppen. They destroyed about 120 aircraft on the ground including seven Sparrows of 'D' Flight. Newton Foster says they were taken completely by surprise and everyone found whatever shelter they could. He and his friend took cover behind some drums. After the raid he found that his friend had been killed and that the drums were full of petrol.

So ended 'D' Flight and the survivors flew back to England to rejoin the squadron. Operational flying now ceased at Doncaster and the airfield was relegated to little more than a lorry park. Ever since the beginning of preparations for 'Overlord', massive convoys had been passing through Doncaster. Strategically sited on the Great North Road, Doncaster became a stopping place for thousands, possible tens of thousands, of vehicles which needed somewhere to park at night - and that somewhere was often the aerodrome. (The convoys were a delight to the same, now larger, small boys who had wanted a souvenir from the crashed Wellington on Bawtry Road. They kept a complete log of all the tanks, guns etc that passed through town, providing the convoys went through after school hours and it wasn't raining). Petrol was supplied either at the aerodrome or at a temporary military petrol station at the bottom on Town Moor Avenue at the junction of what was then Grandstand Road. The concrete base can still be seen in the corner of the racecourse car park.

German aerial activity over Doncaster had long since ceased, but there was still to be a nasty surprise. The south of England had suffered from flying bombs from June 1944. Towards the end of that year a few of these bombs, launched from German aircraft over the North Sea, reached Doncaster. Mainly at night, people heard the peculiar throb of the 'Doodlebugs' and, uncharitably, hoped that the noise wouldn't stop. If the noise did stop, it meant that the bomb was about to crash land with its load of about one ton of high explosive. None fell in the immediate area of Doncaster. One group of men, however, thought that the noise was the beginning of their salvation, that the secret weapons that their Fuhrer had promised had finally arrived and that the war would soon end in their favour. These (temporarily) happy souls were, of course, the German prisoners of war in their camp at the racecourse. So happy were they that on Christmas Eve, 1944, after some of the flying bombs had gone over, they paraded round the camp perimeter singing 'Deutschland, Deutschland Über Alles'. The guards were sufficiently alarmed to focus searchlights on and to fire over the heads of the prisoners. The singing and the joy were short-lived.

Incidentally, the prisoners still at Doncaster when the war ended were moved to various other camps and were eventually demobbed from the Wehrmacht at Harrogate. They were offered the choice of returning to Germany or staying in Britain. Some chose to stay and today, nearly 50 years later, some of the prisoners are still living in Doncaster.

CHAPTER 4
1945-1992

After the end of the war, CL Air Surveys took over the two pre-war hangars and used them for converting Halifaxes and Ansons to civilian use. The Halifaxes had a freight pannier built into the bomb bay and the

Ansons were restructured to carry passengers. Only about six of each were modified. For about a year, four white-painted Halifaxes were parked in front of the hangars, just behind Doncaster Rovers football ground, and became a bit of a local land-mark.

Handley Page Halifax after being converted to a freighter at Doncaster 1946 L. A. Clark

Some of the 24 Tiger Moths of 9 Reserve Flying School at Doncaster August 1951 L. A. Clark

In October 1947, No 9 Reserve Flying Training School was formed at Doncaster to provide training for RAF reservists. It was equipped with Tiger Moths, Prentices, Oxfords and Ansons. The Prentices were later replaced by Chipmunks. The Prentices were then sold to Aviation Traders of Southend, a company owned by Freddie Laker, later Sir Freddie, where with other Prentices from different parts of the country, they were to be converted into small passenger-carrying aircraft. However, out of over 200, only a handful were actually modified. The Ansons and the Oxfords continued to be used for navigational training.

The conversion from Prentices to Chipmunks was not universally approved. John Maples, one of the instructors, found them cramped, unlike the Prentice which was more like a bus, with plenty of room.

Ansons of 9 Reserve Flying School August 1951 L. A. Clark

Kirby Kite of 24 Gliding School
after an inspection by Air Commodore
Gillmore CBE, AOC 64 Group July 1949.
John Maples is on the left. St Cecilia's Road in
background   John Maples

Reservists were required to do 40 hours flying a year and to attend a 14 day summer camp. It was a similar set-up to that of the pre-war Volunteer Reserve - all the fun of flying plus pay. The flying school operated throughout the week with regular RAF officers as instructors.

Before long, further RAF activity came to Doncaster when in January No. 24 Gliding School arrived from Firbeck to train Air Training Corps (ATC) cadets. This was mainly a week-end and holiday activity, and a number of the instructors were also on the staff of the Flying Training School. The old control tower was used for lectures and as an indoor training school. The Gliding School moved to Lindholme in July 1950, and the Reserve Flying Training School was disbanded when the RAF finally left Doncaster in January 1954.

Kite, Cadet MkII and 3 Cadets 1
of No 24 Gliding School, June 1948   J. M. Maples

Before the war, from the opening of the airport, the race meetings had attracted a growing number of aircraft. Numbers reached a peak in 1938. After the war, racegoers' aircraft returned in even greater numbers. Possibly the largest number was in 1949, when the RAF was again running the airfield. Men employed by No 9 Reserve Flying School acted as marshals. Many of the aircraft were

DH86b and DH89 Rapides with other
visiting aircraft at St. Leger 1949   L. A. Clark

Rapides and Dakotas, some operating a shuttle service from places such as Blackpool and Manchester. In later years, the number fell and the type of aircraft changed, the

Rapides and Dakotas giving way to smaller private aircraft. Many if not most of them carried jockeys and trainers. For a number of years, horses were also flown in, sometimes in Bristol Freighters.

Grumman Mallard amphibian belonging to Maharaja of Baroda visiting Doncaster races September 1950. L. A. Clark

In 1960, civil flying started again, this time without engines, when Doncaster and District Gliding Club came into being. The Club had been formed in 1959 after a series of meetings held first at the Trades Club in Doncaster and then at the Brown Cow, a public house on the North Bridge where Jim Durdy had gathered a group of like-minded enthusiasts. From these small beginnings, with members paying half a crown at each meeting, there emerged a gliding club that was before long to become one of the largest in the North of England. The club leased some buildings on the airfield from Doncaster County Borough Council at a peppercorn rent of about £50 per year. This rent also covered the use of the airfield for gliding.

The outer part of the wing of a Canberra bomber which exploded in mid-air over Doncaster in 1951. The wing fell onto a house in Waverley Road, Balby, the major part fnto a school playground at Edlington and other parts as far afield as the airfield at Doncaster

Since the departure of the RAF, the whole place had been left to the mercies of local vandals and the buildings the Gliding Club took over needed a great deal of work to make them usable. The former guard room and the mortuary, both on the Bessacarr side of the railway, were taken over as a club house and workshops. The club's first aircraft came in a rather strange way. The wings were acquired from a scrap merchant in Sprotborough and the fuselage from somewhere else, no-one quite knows where. The parts were put together in the club's workshops, under the leadership of Johnnie Johnson. Other necessary equipment materialised thanks to the good offices of other members. The winch was based on a Bedford

Glider being towed home after mistaking the racecourse for the airfield   Harry Keeble

chassis, with the drum containing the tow rope powered by the lorry's engine. It might seem a bit amateurish but everything had to be completed to the satisfaction of the British Gliding Association - and was.

Flying started with the completed glider, called a Cadet, a basic single seater, so the first flights could only be made by qualified pilots. However before long the club acquired a T31, a two seat training aircraft. Now all members had the opportunity of flying, and training started in earnest. The club had attracted a number of very experienced pilots and instructors. More members joined and more aircraft were acquired. By the late sixties, the membership had grown to over 200. One member, Frank Haigh, had a Tiger Moth which he lent, at times, to the club to be used as a tug, offering tows to members. Frank Haigh lived next to the airfield, so he could keep his aircraft at the bottom of the garden, suitably tied down (it was close to the spot where the Harrow had been blown over in December 1940). Unfortunately Frank Haigh had a serious accident on the airfield when a passenger taking photographs accidentally let a piece of his equipment fall into the controls.

Other powered aircraft were made available to the club, including an Auster belonging to Jack Tarr and Jack Bower, both of them local businessmen.

Budding glider pilots 1965   G. H. Oakes

In 1968, the club was chosen to be the host of the National Gliding Championship, an honour that showed the thoroughness with which the club was organised and operated.

National Gliding Championships at Doncaster 1968   *G. H. Oakes*

Except for a couple of years from 1949 to about 1951, there had been no official civilian powered-flying since before the war. In 1949, Doncaster Ultra Light Aircraft Association had operated out of the Rollason hangar, by kind permission of the RAF, first with an Avro Tutor - which crashed. The next aircraft was a BA Swallow, the type used by the pre-war flying club. Instructors were often from No 9 Reserve Flying Training School.

BA Swallow rescued by Tony Clark from a garage in Gainsborough and rebuilt in   *L. A. Clark*
his garden at Belle Vue then hangared for a while at Doncaster by kind permission of the RAF.
In the background are the two pre-war hangars and the Ministry of Aircraft Production factory

The possibility of using the airfield for powered-flying was appreciated by a number of local people and quiet approaches were made to Doncaster County Borough Council into the prospects of reopening the site as a proper airfield for light aircraft. The response was encouraging, so much so that a company was formed, South Yorkshire Airport (Doncaster) Ltd, by a number of local business men, Ernest Crabtree (who was Chairman), Jack Bower from the Gliding club, John Bingham and Geoffrey Oakes. Harry Keeble took the place of Jack Bower (who tragically died) and John Hall took the place of John Bingham when he resigned. The Gliding Club had been the sole user of the airfield for a number of years but they welcomed their possible new neighbours.

Although a company had been formed and there were helpful signs from the council, there was still a long way to go. People had to be shown that the new company was able to operate the airfield. To this end, the company invited the Council leader, Councillor R. Bowes, to take a flight over Doncaster. Like most people seeing Doncaster from the air for the first time, he was amazed how green it looked. As he was enjoying his flight, and since it was a pleasant day, it was suggested that they take a trip to the coast. Half-way there, the important passenger went to sleep. Nevertheless it was decided to carry on. As they approached the coast, dark rain clouds were seen in front and although the plane could have climbed over the clouds, it was thought unwise to worry Councillor Bowes by having him shaken up by rough weather and the plane turned for home. Councillor Bowes woke up just before they arrived home, said how much he had enjoyed the flight and that he was a supporter. As he left the airfield, the rain started.

Avro Tutor operated by the Ultra Light Aircraft Group   Bruce/Leslie
before it crashed in 1950. On the wing tip is Frank Haigh

Following the successful flight with Councillor Bowes, another trip was arranged for leading councillors and council officers. This time the destination was the Leeds/Bradford Airport where the Chairman, Ernest Crabtree, had a large aviation company. They flew in two twin-engined aircraft. Before the flight started, the captain of the aircraft in which the Town Clerk, Mr. V. Douglas Knox, was flying learnt that he had been a bomber pilot during the war. It seemed a good idea to offer him an opportunity to take the controls. So, it was arranged that he would have the seat next to the pilot. As the passengers got on board, Mr. Knox, as ever a gentleman, offered his seat to the Mayor which he duly took. The pilot had not been informed of the change and half way to Leeds, he sat back with his hands off the controls and said, "Over to you". The first citizen of Doncaster does not panic. He quietly pointed out that he had no idea of what to do and would the pilot please do his job, saying all this of course in a pleasant conversational sort of way. Whilst the party was looking round the building at Leeds, the senior pilot checked the weather for the return journey. It was not too good. However Air Traffic Control at Finningley promised help with radar. Under their guidance the aircraft returned to Doncaster but as they could only give them instructions to land at Finningley, the two aircraft had to make an approach to that station. It so happened that it was the day of Finningley's Battle of Britain celebrations. So the two aircraft flew down the main runway watched by the thousands waiting for the annual display. At the end of the runway they turned right and flew along the Great North Road and landed safely at Doncaster.

There was some competition from another company, but in September 1967 the South Yorkshire Airport Company signed a ten-year lease on the airport at a rent of £50 per year. The lease did not cover the entire airfield. There was still a possibility that the M18 might be built through it and across the racecourse. Until the route had been finally agreed, the council had to reserve the land that might be required and only gave the airport company a 'Licence to operate' over the possible route.

There were still many problems to overcome before flying could start. Perhaps the major problem was the fact that the RAF did not like the idea of private flying close to Lindholme and Finningley. The Civil Aviation Authority were perfectly happy for flying to start at the new airfield and they gave all the help they could - to no avail.

To resolve the impasse a conference was called at Lindholme. On the appointed day, the Chairman, appointed by the CAA, first had a meeting with representatives of the airport company and explained to them that they had every right to operate and not to be intimidated by the RAF. At Lindholme the company's representatives were shown into a large board room with an imposing conference table. Sitting round the table was a phalanx of senior RAF officers, none lower than squadron leader and others somewhat higher. It soon became apparent that every hurdle was to be put in front of the Doncaster opening. The chairman pointed out that the RAF could not stop it and it was in the RAF's interest that the airfield should operate efficiently. It was finally agreed that the RAF would give radar help to aircraft inbound to Doncaster and a direct phone link would be established between control towers. The airspace was shared out, with powered aircraft from Doncaster operating to the north and the gliding club to the south of Doncaster. The RAF would whenever possible keep to the south of Finningley.

In reality it was not surprising that the RAF were reluctant. The thought of a lost Auster wandering across Finningley when a squadron of Vulcans was being scrambled in response to a 'Four Minute Warning' would not be something the Air Staff would view with favour. The atmosphere had been tense but when the chairman closed the meeting, everything changed. The RAF officers explained that they had been ordered by even more senior officers to oppose the airfield and they apologised for what they had been forced to say. Both sides went into the bar and the day ended with everyone on the best of terms.

Several parts of the airfield had been let to other users. One of them was Doncaster United, a local amateur football team, who used the control tower as a club house and had their pitch on the other side of the apron. Agreement was reached with their chairman, Ronnie Massarella (who was, among much else, Team Manager of the British International and Olympic Show Jumping team) and the club moved to another pitch provided by the local authority.

The airfield was re-opened by the Mayor of Doncaster with over 100 private aircraft attending and the visitors being fed fresh lobster and other delicacies. The goodies had been flown in by one of the company's directors who had put the lobsters in boxes on the back seat of the aircraft. Something went wrong and as he turned round he was horrified to see live lobsters crawling about his feet.

To control this mass of aircraft, a professional Air Traffic Controller was brought in from Manchester Airport, though the aids he had at his disposal were very basic, just radio.

Stampes of the Rothmans aerobatic team at Doncaster 1969   G. H. Oakes

The 'second' opening was in May, 1968. The celebratory display was organised by the Tiger Club of Redhill and was almost indistinguishable from the displays held before the war - balloons bursting, flour-bomb dropping, aerobatics with biplanes and many other skillful acts all with rather old fashioned aircraft. One of the highlights was the performance of Susan Cherry who stood on the wing of a Tiger Moth and armed with a pole burst a long row of balloons as she flew past them. She had never done anything of the kind before but she was totally successful and the company was very grateful - even though she had refused to wear a bathing costume. In keeping with tradition more than half of the estimated crowd of 10,000 stayed outside the airfield and so escaped paying.

The control tower was modernised with the installation of a direction finder unit. With this equipment, the controller at the airport was able to give the directions an aircraft needed to reach the airfield. In capable hands it could give directions to incoming aircraft in bad weather. On top of the control tower was built a 'greenhouse' where the controller could see the entire airfield. It was here that the CR/DF unit was installed. The middle floor was used as offices and a classroom. The ground floor was converted into a club house, run by Grace Tarr. Later it was turned into a night club run by Mr. Innes, who lived in the bungalow which had been used as a club house by the pre-war flying club. A flat over one of the garages had been renovated for use by one of the aircraft engineers.

The two runways were laid out in true RAF style, one NE/SW and the other NW/SE. The Sommerfeld tracking laid by the RAF 18 years earlier had started to break up and a daily check had to be made to ensure there were no exposed pieces of metal. Both pre-war hangars were brought back into use, although the huge doors of the Rollason hangar presented problems.

With the reopening of the airfield, the South Yorkshire Flying Club was formed. It had two Cessnas, a 150 and a 172. Further Cessnas followed and they were joined by Rollason Condors, a throwback to pre-war days. A permanent staff was appointed to run both the airport and flying club. An ex-RAF instructor, Jim Watson, joined the staff as Chief Flying Instructor and the first student to gain her private pilot's licence at the club was Janet Claybourn, wife of the present owner of the Flying Flea.

Jim Watson was unfortunately killed in a tragic accident on the airfield on April 14, 1973 when flying a French-built Jodel. The official report said that the probable cause of the accident had been 'lack of flying speed'. That morning he had been flying a similar aircraft but one with its instrument readings expressed in metric. The second aircraft had its readings in Imperial. It can be assumed that he misread the instruments.

Northair Aviation of Leeds used the airfield to provide air-taxi facilities. Its first charter predated the airfield's official re-opening and as early as November 2, 1967, a Piper Aztec of Northair Aviation had flown Brian Livingston, Technical Director of Rockware Glass of Doncaster with several other company executives, on a trip to Prestwick in Scotland.

Jim Watson, first Chief Flying Instructor of South Yorkshire Flying Club. Killed at Doncaster in a flying accident on 14th April 1973 when flying a French built Jodel

Wendy Mills

Shortly after the airport's re-opening - and after a lot of heavy rain - a huge depression appeared near the end of the main NE/SW runway and the ground became very waterlogged. The problem was caused by mining subsidence. Even to begin to solve the problem, a great deal of fill was needed. The need coincided with the demolishing of the old Guildhall (formerly the Police Station) in French Gate and its imposing facade of classical pillars. The rubble was used to help stabilise the ground. A heavy-duty grader was then brought in to level the land and the site covered with top soil. But the area did not return to its original state and the runway had to be slightly realigned. If, in a hundred years time, some archaeologists excavating the site of the old Dome come across some classical pillars they might, in their excitement, think they have come across an unknown Roman Villa.

The rest of the landing surface, which in the thirties had been so highly regarded, had deteriorated badly, partly because of further mining subsidence and partly because of general settlement of the old tip infilling which had been used when the airport had first been laid out. The Civil Aviation Authority (CAA) made a yearly inspection of both the airfield and its safety facilities. The CAA inspector was concerned with the condition of the runways. To solve the problem the board agreed to look into the possibility of providing a hard runway. The cost of providing even a small runway for light aircraft was very high and an approach was made to the army to see if they could help - under an 'Aid to the Civil Community' scheme.

Much to the surprise of the airport company, the Royal Engineers at York were very enthusiastic. They had a site on Salisbury Plain where one of

Pitts S2 Specials aerobatic team   *Barry Thomson*

their units had built a runway - as practice for building runways in some undeveloped corner of the world. Then another unit came along and ripped it up. The chance of building a real runway that would be actually used was too good to be missed. The company would pay for the materials and the army would provide the manpower and planning. The company had to seek permission of all the unions that might have been involved in the building and also the companies that might have been given the contract. Everyone agreed with the idea and in 1970 an application was made for planning permission for a runway of 1,000 yards plus associated taxi ways. The application was turned down. One councillor objected to the thought of Boeing 707s landing day and night, and no one was able to persuade him that is was impossible for aircraft of that size to use the runway. Others thought the airport catered for 'elitist hobbies'.

When the news got around that Doncaster was planning a hard runway, the company had many enquiries about bringing business to the town, not only from companies involved in aviation but others looking for a site near an airfield that could accommodate business aircraft. These included a company that wanted to build golfing buggies for clients who would want to come by air. Another firm exported plant and equipment all over Europe and had to be able to get anywhere in 24 hours to repair breakdowns. The firm's aircraft would be based at Doncaster and a large spares store would be built on or near the airfield. Altogether there were about 15 companies who wanted to come, but without the hard runway their interest melted away. The lack of planning permission was a death knell for both the company and the airfield though the airfield would be a long time in dying. But die it did, in just another 20 years.

Before the war Doncaster had gained a lot of publicity for its air shows - from the original in 1909 to the Empire Air Displays and Pageants of the 1930s. The display held to celebrate the reopening had been comparatively small, but it was agreed that a display with modern aircraft would be organised as part of the 1970 IMPEL week. ('IMPEL' weeks were organised mainly by the Chamber of Commerce to allow local businesses and organisations to put on displays. There was a big parade through the town. Three IMPEL weeks were held at that time at three yearly intervals.) Approaches were made, first to the RAF, and then to the American Air Force in the UK. The RAF were very professional and promised a number of aircraft including the Red Arrows, though the airport company would have to cover them for insurance. How do you cover the Red Arrows for £1 million? In the end it was simple. There is a company that covered most if not all the Red Arrows displays for about £100.

The Americans were very different. After speaking to a number of officers, an airport director was put through to a major who played the part of the shop assistant nonchalantly selling hardware. Do you want a pair of Phantoms? How about a F111? And so on. In the end a shopping list was agreed worth millions. The only refusal was to the request for the C5 GALAXY which was on its first flight to Europe. The major said it was outside his control. The Galaxy was and still is the biggest aircraft in the western world and because it was designed to land and take off from fairly short unprepared strips it could have operated out of Doncaster. Unfortunately, a few weeks later, the Americans had to withdraw because of an exercise in Germany.

On the Wednesday before the display, a practice was held with the press and TV present, plus a number of invited spectators. The afternoon went well, except that the teachers in the schools at the bottom of Sandy Lane complained that the events on the airfield had disturbed the children who paid more attention to the aircraft than to their lessons.

Several VIPs were invited to the display, including the Mayor of Doncaster and the Station Commander from Finningley. The Station Commander had invited one of the airport directors to the last two Finningley air displays, sent his own escort to the gate to greet him, provided a ring-side seat in an easy chair in front of the crowd and just behind the Chief of the Air Staff with his red phone in case of a 'Four Minute Warning' and had a junior officer serve raspberries and cream washed down with wine. At Doncaster, the Finningley Station Commander was given a hard folding chair and a cup of tea out of a plastic cup. It was the best that could be done, but the Station Commander was full of praise for the display.

Besides the modern aircraft, there were flights by a number of ancient biplanes - "<u>real</u> flying" said the Station Commander. The display ended with the Gnats of the Red Arrows flying low over Bawtry Road, streaming red white and blue smoke to such an extent that drivers on the main road could not see where they were going. There was chaos for minutes but luckily no accidents. The police chief in the tower was showered with complaints from his officers on traffic duty. In keeping with tradition more people watched outside the airfield than paid.

Concern was expressed, though not by the children, that aircraft using the shorter NW/SE runway might be a danger to the schools at the bottom of Sandy Lane. To prove that their fears were unfounded, the local MP, Harold Walker, later Sir Harold, was invited for a flight using the short runway. The Chairman of the company, using one of his twin-engined aircraft, took off and pretended that one of the engines failed on take off, a most dangerous situation. He went through the recovery programme and the aircraft, apparently without any trouble, landed safely.

Before going into the club house for a drink, the pilot confided to another of the passengers that it had not been just an exercise, the engine really had failed and the recovery programme had been for real, as was the sweat! Harold Walker was not told at the time and he remained ignorant for the next 20 years. After the flight he agreed that the schools were in no danger, but to be extra safe the direction of the runway was slightly changed.

The Flying Club had reached such a standard that a contract was won from the Air Ministry to train ATC cadets to a standard just below the point when they would get their private pilot's licence. The cadets were housed in accommodation that was specially erected by the control tower.

The club's aircraft strength had increased to about seven. In addition, there were up to 20 private aircraft belonging to club members plus other aircraft that were hangared at Doncaster. After the problems with the air display in 1970, the airport resisted pleas to hold another but the club held a number of social weekends with a number of visiting aircraft and competitions. But they were not open to the general public.

The lack of a hard runway effectively barred any development of the airfield and it was now just a question of serving out the rest of the lease. The problem caused by the lack of a hard runway was highlighted when the directors of The National Coal Board were flying in their official aircraft, a Dove, over the airfield, with the control tower in sight but with the ground hidden under a thin layer of fog. It was not possible for the aircraft to land without powerful runway lighting and other aids which would have been in place if a hard runway had been built. It had to divert and the waiting chauffeur-driven cars had to chase them to Leeds.

The problem was further demonstrated when Volkswagen wanted to land their business jet, a DH125, but had to be refused. These were not the only instances, none of them a good advertisement for Doncaster.

The first private aircraft-builders with Doncaster and district connections had been Claybourns, although they only built one aircraft, the pre-war Flying Flea. After the war, there were more, all of them members of the Doncaster Flying Club. First was John Penny of Sheffield who turned part of his house in Sheffield into a workshop, but used Doncaster as his airfield. His first aircraft was an Evans VP1, a low-winged monoplane which had its first flight at Doncaster in 1972. This was followed by a replica of a Sopwith Triplane, one of the most successful British fighters in the first war. It was not an aeroplane to build overnight. It took 17 years from the first inspiration to the first flight.

John built others, but rather more quickly, averaging one every two years. His next aircraft were a Kitfox Mark 2, then an Evans VP2, a two-seater version of the VP1 he had already built and finally a Kitfox Mark 4. There cannot be many people who have personally built five aircraft.

The second of the private builders was George Shield, headmaster of

Mexborough Grammar School. In 1966 he built a Luton Minor, using spare capacity in the school's workshops. Its first flight was at Kirton in Lindsay on January 22, 1967, but the aircraft was based at Doncaster from July 1972. Building an aircraft from other people's plans was not enough of a challenge to George. Next time he decided to do it all himself and design the aircraft from scratch. His approach appears simple: "First what you want the aircraft to do. That gives the outline of the basic design. Add to that the size of a comfortable chair and you're on your way. The principle is - get the mathematics right, everything else follows." One set of equations gave some trouble. So he summoned one of his sixth form mathematics students, sat him down, and told him to solve the problem - which he did. That was another advantage of being the headmaster of the local grammar school - he had brains on call, and of course space.

His aircraft were either totally black or black and white, and if anyone doubted his artistic skill, they would have to be careful - George is a sculptor of note and a number of his creations have been accepted by the Royal Academy for their Summer Exhibition.

Aerial view of Doncaster Aero Club with Doncaster Rovers   Linda Firbank
Football ground and part of Belle Vue.

Home built aircraft by Doncaster Aero Club members

John Penny's homebuilt Kitfox IV similar but larger than the Kitfox II built a little earlier   John Penny

John Penny's homebuilt VPII   John Penny

John Penny's homebuilt Sopwith Triplane, it only took 17 years, with the builder   John Penny
dressed as a World War I fighter pilot with his bike handy in case the engine won't start

Home built aircraft by Doncaster Aero Club members

John Penny's homebuilt VPI

John Penny

Luton Minor, homebuilt in spare corner of school workshop, by George Shield

George Shield

XYLA, homebuilt in spare corner of school workshop, by George Shield

George Shield

Wendy Mills, with half completed Tipsy Nipper 1970   Wendy Mills

The third builder was Wendy Mills, a newspaper reporter and in her spare time a flying instructor. Using a room at the back of the hangar at Doncaster, she built a Tipsy Nipper.

Eight light aircraft built by the members of one club is good building.

The time of South Yorkshire Airport was over, but they granted a sub-

The staff of Doncaster Aero club, with some of their fleet of training aircraft. They are Barry Thomson
Chief Flying Instructor Les Meadows (front), Commercial Manager Linda Firbank (middle right),
Flying Instructor Paul Forster (middle left) Chief Groundsman David Mellows (back right),
Assistant Commercial Manager Gill Lawton (back middle) and trainee Instructor Tim Newman (back left)

Cessna landing at Doncaster, mid eighties, over the site of the old control tower and the present Dome   Barry Thomson

lease to a company called Eastern Aviation. Eastern Aviation, from Sherburn near Leeds, was owned by David Blackburn and Mike Collet, but within weeks Mike Collet left to take up other aviation opportunities and Eastern Aviation gave way to David Blackburn's Flight Line. Besides owning the flying club and the other facilities at the airfield, Flight Line was also Grumman Aviation's UK distributor of their family of light aircraft. At first these small aircraft came in crates from the United States and were reassembled in the hangars at Doncaster but later some were flown in direct, a very long haul across the Atlantic for a single-engined aircraft.

In 1976 Flight Line gave way to the Doncaster Aero Club and the Grumman agency was passed to another company in the south of England.

The Doncaster Aero Club was formed by members taking shares and running it on a non-profit basis. The club stayed until the airfield closed in 1992, but its existence was threatened within months of it taking over. The 1967 lease was for ten years and in early 1976 it was announced that Doncaster Metropolitan Borough Council intended to submit a planning application for 1,300 houses, shops and offices plus recreation facilities on the site. The Secretary of State for the Environment called the application in and set up a public inquiry. Thus started 18 months of conflict, with the local authority pushing their scheme for development and being opposed by the Aero Club and the Gliding Club. The flying fraternity were fortunate to have the services of counsel helped by Wendy Mills of the Aero Club and Joe Millward of the Gliding Club who did the leg work. The Council argued that there was a tremendous demand for housing which could only be met by developing the airfield. The Aero and Gliding Clubs contended that there was not such a demand and what demand there was could easily be met with other sites in the town. They also claimed that the services provided by the clubs were important to the business and leisure life of the town and the racecourse would suffer if jockeys and other racegoers could not land close by. They gave figures of the use made of the airfield by the various businesses and occupations and both clubs showed the impact they made on the recreational life of the town. Nevertheless, it was universally expected that the Council would win. So when in August 1977 the Secretary of State declared in favour of the flying clubs, their joy was as high as the Council's gloom was deep. It was a victory of two Davids over Goliath.

But the problems of the Doncaster Aero Club were far from over. The original 1967 lease had to be renewed in 1977 - which it was for another ten years. It was then made clear that when the new lease expired, the site would have to be returned to the Local Authority. In other words, the club had ten years to persuade the Council to change their minds and to show any doubters of the need for the continuation of the airport.

In 1976 the airport had a strange visitor, an Airship. Howden in East Yorkshire had been the birthplace of the R.100 a competitor to the R.101, which had crashed at Beauvais in 1930, killing amongst others Lord Thomson the Secretary of State for Air. The crash proved to be the death knell of passenger airships in this country and the R.100 which had been designed by Barnes Wallis with the future novelist Nevil Shute as chief engineer was dis-mantled. (Nevil Shute had been involved with the Courier and other aircraft which had been so often seen at Doncaster in pre-war years.) The airship that arrived in 1976 was the Europa, built by Goodyear and operated by them for advertising purposes. It was based in Italy and spent its time travelling around Europe with an Italian aircrew and

Goodyear airship at Doncaster 1976   G. H. Oakes

91

the large ground crew that was needed every time it took off or landed. While at Doncaster, it made many trips carrying Goodyear customers and local VIPs. It was a success. Four years later it returned and on a number of occasions used Doncaster as an overnight stop.

Further trouble came again in 1976 when the second of the pre-war hangars caught fire and three aircraft were destroyed and others damaged. Even this was not the end of the Aero Club's troubles. A short time later, the control tower was also burnt down. Since the departure of the South Yorkshire Flying Club in 1973, the control tower had been used only by the night club and all flying control had been organised from a building beside the second hangar. This building was also used as a social centre for the airfield and the flying club.

In spite of everything, the club thrived and, in 1976, 49 students gained their private pilot's licence and many others upgraded their qualifications. The club operated five training aircraft and another 14 aircraft were based on the airfield, nine of them owned by companies. There was a staff of eleven, four full-time and seven part-time. A further addition to the facilities was a parachuting school. Under fully qualified instructors, people were offered courses in the first of the pre-war hangars. A weekend would be spent in basic instruction. The first jump would cost around £85, subsequent jumps much less, depending on the height from which the jump was made. The average cost would be about £20 including the use of a parachute. With an active membership of over 200, the club was fast becoming one of the biggest in the North of England.

With 1987 approaching, Doncaster Metropolitan Borough Council tried once again to obtain possession of the airfield. They now had specific plans for the area which they didn't have ten years earlier. They wanted

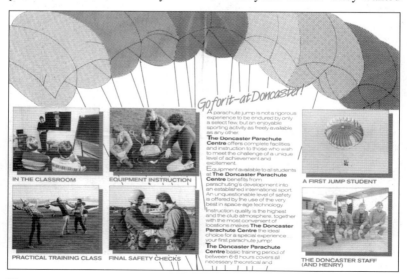

Go for it – at Doncaster!

IN THE CLASSROOM   EQUIPMENT INSTRUCTION   A FIRST JUMP STUDENT

PRACTICAL TRAINING CLASS   FINAL SAFETY CHECKS   THE DONCASTER STAFF (AND HENRY)

Parachuting at Doncaster, a pastime with a future,
if you miss the photographer

Barry Thomson

to build a leisure centre and sell or lease other sites for business. Negotiations between the Doncaster Aero Club and the Council were protracted but the final result was that the Council would grant the club a further extension for five years and help it find an alternative site. Part of the agreement was that the club would vacate the hangars and move to the Ellers Road site, used by the RAF where facilities would be provided similar to the ones vacated on the other side of the airfield. At a cost of over £100,000 a new hangar and other facilities were built and the club moved into their new quarters. It gave up half the airfield and handed it back to the Council. Within days, the two hangars were demolished. The neatherd's house had already gone as had the old club house bungalow and other buildings. The airport of the nineteen thirties had completely disappeared and in its place there was an Asda store, a multi-channel cinema, and much else including what appears to be a gigantic ice cream factory, the Dome, the largest indoor leisure centre in the North.

The final development was in the late nineteen eighties when the Yorkshire Helicopter Centre moved in. The Centre provided helicopters for sale or hire and provided pilot training.

One of the last aircraft to visit Doncaster was a Dakota nearly 60 years after the first Dakota, belonging to KLM, had come to Doncaster on its way from Amsterdam to Liverpool.

On Christmas Day, 1992, Peter Skinner, a director of the Doncaster Aero Club, flew one more flight, the final flight from Doncaster Airport.

THE FUTURE

DMBC

Acknowledgements

Group Captain & Mrs. J.N.Glover

Cresswell Viney

Carl Speddings

Wendy Mills

Buck Casson

Alan Hartley

E.Newton Foster

Ron Williams

Bob Graham

Geoffrey Turner (my nephew)

J.V.Venn

Brenda Mitchell

Frank Lord

Barry Thompson

Ian Lovell

Alan Dobson

Peter Scott

Mr. & Mrs. J. Kilburn

Group Captain Graham Pitchfork

Graham Claybourn

Stanley Sands

W. Woodford

Tom (Max) Williams

Arthur Radcliffe

Eric King

A.J.W.Smith

Harry Keeble

Linda Firbank

Mr. & Mrs. L.A.Clark, particularly for Mr. Clark's encyclopaedic
knowledge of aircraft registration numbers

Mike Goodall, Brooklands Museum

K. Delve

Public Records Office, Kew

Ministry of Defence, Air Historical Branch

Royal Air Force Museum, Hendon

Doncaster Library, Local History Section

Doncaster Museum

Doncaster Borough Archives

Cantley Library

George Smith, Earnshaw Ltd

Peter Batten, Westlands

Sheffield Star

A man on Church Street, Armthorpe

Sir Harold Walker

Bill Woodford

J.M.Maples

Charles E.Jackson

M.Legard

Councillor J.Meredith

David Cuttriss

Joyce Dunn

Ronnie Massarella

My younger son, David

My elder brother, Bryan, who took a raw manuscript
and turned it into the book you see

Alan Childs, Photographer

George Shield

John Penny

G. Wagstaff

Geoff and June Bennett whose eagle eyes read and corrected any
mistakes on the printers proof

D.Bateman

Bruce Robertson

Campbell P. Gunstan

S. Leslie

J. Blaik

Terry Harrison

'After The Battle', 3 New Plaistow Road, London E15 3JA
for letting me use the photograph of the Wellington at the
RAF museum at Hendon.

I hope this list is complete. If anyone is missed out, would he or she
please accept my sincere apologies.